BETTER HOMES AND GARDENS®

GRILL IT RIGHT!

BETTER HOMES AND GARDENS® BOOKS
Des Moines, Iowa

GRILL IT RIGHT!

Editor: Shelli McConnell
Writers: Marlene Brown, Heidi Kaisand, Joyce Trollope, Mary Williams
Graphic Designers: Neoma Thomas, Tom Wegner
Copy Editor: Joanne Johnson
Test Kitchen Product Supervisor: Marilyn Cornelius
Food Stylists: Lynn Blanchard, Pat Godsted, Janet Herwig, Jennifer Peterson
Food Photographers: Mike Dieter, Lyne Neymeyer, Shigeta Associates, William Stites, Joan Vanderschuit

BETTER HOMES AND GARDENS® BOOKS

An Imprint of Meredith® Books
President, Book Group: Joseph J. Ward
Vice President and Editorial Director: Elizabeth P. Rice
Executive Editor: Connie Schrader
Art Director: Ernest Shelton
Prepress Production Manager: Randall Yontz
Production Editor: Paula Forest
Test Kitchen Director: Sharon Stilwell

WE CARE!

All of us at Better Homes and Gardens® Books are dedicated to providing you with
the information and ideas you need to create tasty foods. We welcome your comments
and suggestions. Write us at: Better Homes and Gardens® Books, Cookbook Editorial
Department, BB-117, 1716 Locust St., Des Moines, IA 50309-3023

If you would like to order additional copies of any of our books,
call 1-800-678-2803 or check with your local bookstore.

Our seal assures you that every recipe in *Grill It Right!* has
been tested in the Better Homes and Gardens® Test Kitchen.
This means that each recipe is practical and reliable, and
meets our high standards of taste appeal. We guarantee your
satisfaction with this book for as long as you own it.

INTRODUCTION

As much as we all love foods that are barbecued, along with their irresistible aromas, the actual grilling process can be somewhat intimidating. Given the amazing variety of equipment available for grilling, from diminutive hibachis to state-of-the-art smokers and gas grills, there is a lot to know!

Not only that, but what about all of the other paraphenalia that goes with these outdoor cookers? Should you choose indirect or direct heat? Use a drip pan, or just arrange the coals in a cone-shaped pile? And when it comes to the food you're grilling, should you skewer it, rotisserie it, throw it in a basket, tie it, or wrap it in foil?

If questions like these tempt you to limit your barbecue forays to the occasional burger or hotdog, take a look at the easy-to-follow information and mouth-watering recipes in this book. These pages are filled with sure-fire formulas to get you grilling successfully in no time at all. You'll find all kinds of entrées, and other special delights as well.

We're confident that the easy answers presented in this book will whet your appetite for the delicious American tradition of outdoor cookery!

CONTENTS

FIRE UP THE GRILL

For a taste of Americana, there's nothing like a
backyard barbecue! Whether you're a tong-wielding
novice or an experienced professional, you'll find lots
of invaluable tips on the following pages.
Learn about buying the best equipment, using it safely,
getting the fire started, and enjoying the most
from your grill. Fire up!

At Home on the Barbecue Grill

No one knows exactly when our ancestors discovered that meat placed over a fire became juicy, tender, and very pleasant to eat. The sizzling sensations, flavors, and aromas of barbecued meats have been enjoyed for perhaps 100,000 years or more. Historians tell us that the practice of cooking meat or fish on sticks or twigs has been connected to the Greeks and the nomadic meat-eaters of the Balkan Peninsula and Asia Minor. They also used substantial branches that became the first rotisseries, rotating whole baby lambs and goats over fire.

An American Love Affair
It's not only great taste that has Americans hooked on barbecuing. It's also the fact that grilling outdoors can't be beat for fun and relaxation. The informality of outdoor cookery lends itself perfectly to easy entertaining, plus it gets the cook out of the kitchen.

The Barbecue Industry Association tells us that Americans are grilling every night of the week, on average, five times each month. That totals 2.3 billion barbecues a month!

Grilling for Good Health
Health concerns are first and foremost on our list when it comes to food and cooking. You may have heard about the possible health risks associated with foods cooked over high heat. Barbecuing, broiling at high temperatures, and smoking have all been implicated. However, no scientific study has proven that barbecued foods are real health hazards.

Nutritionists and food research scientists say that high-heat cooking methods, such as barbecuing, can produce minute amounts of harmful substances when fat from meat drips onto hot coals, resulting in flare-ups, flames that come in contact with the food. However, they admit that the possible health risks are very low.

What You Can Do
If you are concerned about grilling foods for health reasons, the Barbecue Industry Association recommends using indirect heat for grilling. This simply means that you place a drip pan under the meat or food you are grilling, banking the hot coals around the drip pan. The fat then drips into the pan, and not onto the hot coals, preventing flare-ups. Using indirect heat as a cooking method is one way to sidestep the potential dangers of barbecuing, however small.

Because of these concerns, wherever possible, we have incorporated both indirect and direct grilling methods in our recipes.

You can also precook meats or other foods before placing them on the grill to shorten cooking time, and raise your grill rack as high as possible over your heat source. It's also another reason to clean your grill thoroughly after each use.

Everything You Always Wanted to Know About Grills

Behind every great outdoor cook lies reliable equipment and a successful fire—elements that are easy to achieve, no matter what your budget or cooking expertise. With a bit of practice, you'll find our grilling fundamentals will light a fire under you!

Selecting your grill

There's no right or wrong choice for grilling; simply choose the cooker you will feel most comfortable using.

Braziers: From the inexpensive version on three legs, to the upscale unit complete with hood, rotisserie, and air vents, this is your basic shallow firebox on legs that's designed for direct heat cooking. No matter how elaborate the brazier, the cooking technique will be the same.

Hibachis: These miniature grills are designed for direct heat cooking methods, and are great for the apartment dweller or the budding barbecuer with just a back step for barbecue space. Small foods, such as hotdogs, burgers, steaks, kabobs, and chicken pieces are well-suited to this grill. Small and portable, most hibachis have grill racks and air vents that are adjustable.

Kettle or Wagon Grills: Designs vary, but these kettle-shaped (or covered-wagon) grills are all designed for closed-hood grilling. Air vents or lid design helps control ventilation; you can choose from charcoal, gas, and electric units. Many have optional accessories, such as shelves that attach to the sides of the grill for easy serving, and hooks or holsters to hold utensils within easy reach. Some even have attachable side-burners that can cook your side dishes while foods finish over the coals.

Water Smokers: Perfect for long, slow cooking, these special covered grills allow you to cook over indirect heat. Dampened wood chunks sprinkled on a fire cook food continuously with steamy clouds of wood smoke for a penetrating barbecue flavor. These are also available in charcoal, gas, and electric models.

Selecting Utensils

Heavy-duty mitts, long-handled tongs, forks, basting brushes, and spatulas are essential for protection from the searing heat of your grill. These utensils come in a pleasing variety of colors and styles; some are even coated with non-stick material for easy clean-up.

Barbecue baskets help keep certain foods, such as fragile fish fillets, small vegetables, and fruits from falling through the grill during cooking. Meat roasting racks mount your roasts and ribs securely to the grill. Corn and potato racks, frankfurter wheels, and kabob skewers are other handy accessories you may want to try.

Preparing the Firebox

If you have a gas or electric grill, follow manufacturer's instructions to get going. Cooking with charcoal? Read your grill's instructions to determine whether the firebox needs to be lined first for protection. Do this with a double layer of heavy foil, then add an inch of pea gravel or coarse grit. This permits better air circulation beneath the coals, so they'll burn more efficiently. For the first dozen uses, this layer will also help prevent flare-ups. To clean, replace the foil; then thoroughly wash and dry the grit bedding.

How Many Briquettes?

A good rule of thumb is to spread coals in a single layer to extend about one inch beyond your food. Add a few more coals if the weather is humid or windy. Once you've "measured" the amount of briquettes needed, push them into a mound for lighting. Several brands of charcoal can be found in markets; experiment to find the kind that works the best for you.

Beyond Charcoal

Wood chips or chunks have become very popular fuels for barbecuing. You can add the chips or chunks to burning briquettes to achieve a special wood-smoked aroma and flavor in barbecued foods. Use wood chunks along with briquettes for fires that will need to burn long and constant. Such woods as mesquite, alder, hickory, oak, and fruitwoods like apple, cherry, and peach are especially good choices for chips or chunks. Read the package labels; chances are the chips will need to be soaked first before you use them. That way, they'll smoke, not flame.

If you have a gas grill, try the new charcoal-flavored briquettes for gas grills. These contain hardwoods such as mesquite or hickory, and impart a real wood-smoked taste and aroma to your barbecue.

Using Fire Starters

Self-lighting briquettes don't require a fire-starter; simply light them with a match to start. To jump-start other types of coals, try an electric starter or a liquid, wax-type (solid), or jelly starter. Consider also a portable (or chimney) starter. Whatever type of starter you select, read the manufacturer's instructions carefully. Wait about a minute after adding a liquid, wax, or jelly starter before igniting coals. Never add more starter after fire has started—and never use gasoline or kerosene to start your coals!

Starting the Grill

Once your coals are ignited, you can go for the burn! Expect self-lighting coals to burn for 5 to 10 minutes before they're ready for grilling; standard briquettes take about 20 to 30 minutes. Coals will appear ash gray in daylight, or glowing red all over at night when they're ready to use.

Arranging The Coals

Before you arrange the coals, you must decide between direct and indirect cooking methods. Direct cooking means placing the food on the grill rack directly over the coals. With long-handled tongs, spread the hot coals evenly in a single layer. You can reduce flare-ups by spreading coals about a half-inch apart.

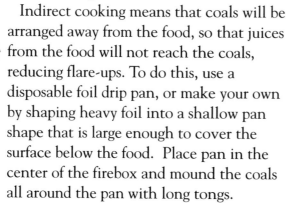

Indirect cooking means that coals will be arranged away from the food, so that juices from the food will not reach the coals, reducing flare-ups. To do this, use a disposable foil drip pan, or make your own by shaping heavy foil into a shallow pan shape that is large enough to cover the surface below the food. Place pan in the center of the firebox and mound the coals all around the pan with long tongs.

Each recipe in this book will refer you to either one or both of these methods.

How Hot Is Hot?

You'll need to be able to judge the hotness of the burning coals, because not all foods are grilled at the same temperature. Hold your hand, palm side down, where your food will cook and at the same height as the food will be grilled. Count by saying, "one thousand-one, one thousand-two", etc. for each second you can hold your hand there. You'll need to remove your hand after two seconds if the coals are hot; three seconds for medium-hot, four for medium, five seconds for medium-slow, and six or more for a slow fire.

Note that for indirect heat cooking, you'll need hot coals to provide medium-hot heat; medium-hot coals for medium heat, medium coals for medium-slow heat, and so forth.

Keeping the Fire Under Control

It's one thing to start a fire; quite another to control it so that you achieve the results you want. You may find that meat juices dripping onto coals cause excessive flare-ups that burn your meat beyond recognition. Try raising the grill rack, covering the grill, arranging the coals with a half-inch of space in between, or removing some of the coals. For severe flare-ups, remove the food from the grill while you mist the flames with a water-spray bottle. Once the flames die down, you can resume the grilling.

Clean-Up & Care of the Grill

It's an excellent idea to clean your grill right after cooking. Let the rack cool slightly. Soak the grill rack and utensils right away in hot sudsy water to loosen cooked-on grime while you enjoy your barbecue. A rack that's too large for your sink can be wrapped in wet paper towels or newspaper; let stand for about an hour. It will be a simple matter to wipe it clean after dinner. If necessary, use a stiff scrub brush (some are made especially for grill-cleaning) to remove stubborn burned-on food. Your manufacturer may also recommend that certain abrasive cleaners not be used, to protect the surface of your grill rack.

YESTERYEAR'S BEST

If your preference for barbecue leans toward all-American favorites, this chapter is for you! Look back to recipes from the '40s to the '80s, and you'll find fifty years' worth of succulent favorites culled from our "best of the best" barbecue recipes!

All-American Burgers

Indirect or Direct Grilling   Serves 4

Sauce:	1	clove garlic, minced, *or* 2 tablespoons finely chopped onion
	2	tablespoons catsup
	1	tablespoon steak sauce
	1	tablespoon Worcestershire sauce
	1	teaspoon sugar
	1	teaspoon cooking oil
	1	teaspoon vinegar
		Few dashes bottled hot pepper sauce
Meat Mixture:	1	pound lean ground beef
	¼	teaspoon salt
	¼	teaspoon pepper
Bread:	4	hamburger buns
Toppings:		American cheese slices (optional)
		Lettuce leaves (optional)
		Tomato slices (optional)
		Red onion slices (optional)
		Pickle slices (optional)

For Sauce: In a small saucepan combine all sauce ingredients. Bring to boiling; reduce heat. Simmer, uncovered, for 5 minutes. Remove from heat; set aside.

To Prepare Meat Mixture: In a medium mixing bowl combine all meat mixture ingredients and mix well. Shape meat mixture into four ¾-inch-thick patties.

To Cook by Indirect Grill Method: In a covered grill arrange preheated coals around a drip pan. Test for *medium* heat above the pan. Place meat on the grill rack over the drip pan. Cover and grill for 20 to 24 minutes or till no pink remains, turning once halfway through grilling time and brushing frequently with sauce.

To Cook by Direct Grill Method: Grill meat on the grill rack of an uncovered grill directly over *medium* coals for 14 to 18 minutes or till no pink remains, turning once halfway through grilling time and brushing frequently with sauce.

To Serve: Split and toast the buns on the grill. Serve patties in buns with cheese, lettuce, tomato, onion, and pickle, if desired.

Thick, juicy burgers topped the list of food hits in the '40s, just as they do today.

Per serving: 327 calories / 24 g protein / 25 g carbohydrate / 14 g fat (5 g saturated) / 71 mg cholesterol / 611 mg sodium / 304 mg potassium.

Grilled Franks with Lots of Barbecue Sauce

Indirect or Direct Grilling   Serves 8

Sauce:	1	15-ounce can tomato sauce
	½	cup chopped onion (1 medium)
	1	tablespoon sugar
	1	tablespoon lemon juice
	1	teaspoon Worcestershire sauce
		Dash pepper
		Few dashes bottled hot pepper sauce
Meat:	1	16-ounce package (8) frankfurters
Bread:	8	frankfurter buns, split

When you dunk plump and juicy franks in a zippy sauce like this, no other sandwich fixin's are needed.

For Sauce: In a medium saucepan combine all sauce ingredients. Bring to boiling; reduce heat. Cover and simmer about 30 minutes or till onion is tender. Remove from heat; set aside.

To Cook by Indirect Grill Method: In a covered grill arrange preheated coals around a drip pan. Test for *medium* heat above the pan. Place frankfurters on the grill rack over the drip pan. Cover and grill for 10 to 12 minutes or till heated through.

To Cook by Direct Grill Method: Grill frankfurters on the grill rack of an uncovered grill directly over *medium-high* coals for 3 to 5 minutes or till frankfurters are heated through, turning occasionally.

To Serve: Dip grilled frankfurters in the sauce and place in buns. If desired, serve with additional sauce.

The '40s

GI's returning from the war were greeted by families who were hungry for barbecue. Because portable grills were not yet available, these enthusiasts built fireplace-size brick ovens in the backyard and bought basic grilling tools—long-handled forks, tongs, and brushes. Recipes then were designed to ensure beginners's success: burgers, frankfurters, and juicy charbroiled steaks.

Per serving: 323 calories / 11 g protein / 28 g carbohydrate / 19 g fat (7 g saturated) / 28 mg cholesterol / 1,204 mg sodium / 352 mg potassium.

Herb-Rubbed Steak

Herb-Rubbed Steak

Indirect or Direct Grilling   Serves 8

Seasoning Rub:	4	cloves garlic, minced
	½	cup finely chopped onion (1 medium)
	1	to 2 teaspoons dried herb, crushed (such as thyme, basil, oregano, rosemary, or Italian seasoning)
	1	teaspoon salt
	¼	teaspoon pepper
Meat:	1	2- to 2½-pound boneless beef sirloin steak, cut 1 to 1½ inches thick
Sauce:		Bottled barbecue sauce (optional)

A good steak needs little seasoning, as this original recipe from the '40s shows. Serve it with a steaming baked potato, julienne carrots, green beans, and additional barbecue sauce.

For Seasoning Rub: In a small mixing bowl combine all seasoning rub ingredients.

To Prepare Meat: Trim fat from steak. Rub seasoning mixture onto both sides of meat.

To Cook by Indirect Grill Method: In a covered grill arrange preheated coals around a drip pan. Test for *medium* heat above the pan. Place meat on the grill rack over the drip pan. Cover and grill to desired doneness (see chart), turning once halfway through grilling time. If desired, brush occasionally with barbecue sauce the last 10 minutes of grilling.

To Cook by Direct Grill Method: Grill steak on the grill rack of an uncovered grill directly over *medium* coals to desired doneness (see chart), turning once halfway through grilling time. If desired, brush occasionally with barbecue sauce the last 10 minutes of grilling.

Doneness		Direct	Indirect
1"	Rare	14 to 18 minutes	22 to 26 minutes
	Medium	18 to 22 minutes	26 to 30 minutes
1½"	Rare	32 to 36 minutes	30 to 36 minutes
	Medium	36 to 40 minutes	36 to 40 minutes

Per serving: 207 calories / 26 g protein / 1 g carbohydrate / 10 g fat (4 g saturated) / 76 mg cholesterol / 323 mg sodium / 365 mg potassium.

Shashlik *(see recipe, page 19)*

Chinese Smoked Ribs
(see recipe, page 22)

Zesty Barbecued Chicken

Zesty Barbecued Chicken

Indirect or Direct Grilling   Serves 4

Sauce:	2	tablespoons margarine *or* butter
	2	tablespoons prepared horseradish
	2	tablespoons catsup
	2	tablespoons vinegar
	1	tablespoon lemon juice
	1	tablespoon Worcestershire sauce
	½ to ¾	teaspoon bottled hot pepper sauce
Poultry:	1	2½- to 3-pound broiler-fryer chicken, quartered

For a summertime picnic, serve slices of cooling cucumber, rings of fresh onion, and a loaf of crusty bread along with this spunky grilled chicken.

For Sauce: In a small saucepan combine all sauce ingredients. Bring to boiling, stirring occasionally. Remove from heat; set aside.

To Prepare Poultry: If desired, remove skin from chicken. Rinse chicken; pat dry.

To Cook by Indirect Grill Method: In a covered grill arrange preheated coals around drip pan. Test for *medium* heat above the pan. Place chicken, bone side down, on the grill rack over the drip pan. Cover and grill for 50 to 60 minutes or till chicken is tender and no longer pink, brushing frequently with sauce the last 10 minutes of grilling.

To Cook by Direct Grill Method: Place the chicken, bone side up, on the grill rack of an uncovered grill. Grill directly over *medium* coals for 40 to 50 minutes or till the chicken

is tender and no longer pink, turning once halfway through grilling time and brushing frequently with the sauce the last 10 minutes of grilling.

The '50s

For young families in the '50s, life revolved around the home. The backyard became the ultimate playground, even for Dad, who proclaimed himself the resident outdoor chef. His whole kit and kaboodle of barbecue equipment—portable grills, skewers, tongs, grill carts, rotisseries, and baskets—made grilling easier and more fun. Skewers meant that any kind of meat or vegetable could become a kabob. Adventuresome families added chicken, ribs, and even fish to their growing repertoire of grilled favorites.

Per serving: 339 calories / 31 g protein / 4 g carbohydrate / 21 g fat (5 g saturated) / 98 mg cholesterol / 362 mg sodium / 312 mg potassium.

Warren's Barbecued Ribs

Rotisserie or Indirect Grilling   Serves 4

Sauce:	1	cup water
	1	cup catsup
	3	tablespoons vinegar
	1	tablespoon sugar
	1	tablespoon Worcestershire sauce
	1	teaspoon celery seed
	¼	teaspoon bottled hot pepper sauce
Meat:	4	pounds pork loin back ribs *or* meaty spareribs (2 strips)

Originally, in the '50s, this wonderfully tangy barbecue sauce was brushed on ribs. More recently, we've found it to be a tasty addition to burgers, chicken, chops, and steaks, too.

For Sauce: In a medium saucepan combine all sauce ingredients. Bring to boiling; reduce heat. Simmer, uncovered, for 30 minutes, stirring occasionally. Remove sauce from heat; set aside.

To Prepare Meat: Sprinkle ribs lightly with *salt* and *pepper*.

To Cook by Indirect Rotisserie Method: Lace ribs, accordion style, onto a spit rod, securing with holding forks. Test the balance. In a covered grill arrange preheated coals around a drip pan. Test for *medium* heat where the meat will be. Attach spit, turn on the motor, and lower the grill hood. Let ribs rotate over drip pan for 1¼ to 1½ hours or till ribs are tender and no pink remains, brushing with sauce the last 15 minutes of grilling. To serve, remove the meat from the spit. Pass any additional sauce.

To Cook by Indirect Grill Method: In a covered grill arrange preheated coals around a drip pan. Test for *medium* heat above the pan. Place ribs on the grill rack over the drip pan. Cover and grill for 1¼ to 1½ hours or till ribs are tender and no pink remains, brushing with sauce the last 15 minutes of grilling. Pass any additional sauce.

Per serving: 783 calories / 52 g protein / 21 g carbohydrate / 54 g fat (21 g saturated) / 214 mg cholesterol / 918 mg sodium / 902 mg potassium.

Shashlik

Indirect or Direct Grilling	Marinating Time: 6 to 24 hours	Serves 6

Marinade:	½ cup chopped onion (1 medium)
	¼ cup snipped parsley
	¼ cup olive oil *or* cooking oil
	¼ cup lemon juice
	1 teaspoon dried marjoram, crushed
	1 teaspoon dried thyme, crushed
	½ teaspoon pepper
	¼ teaspoon salt
	1 clove garlic, minced
Meat:	1½ pounds lean boneless leg of lamb *or* beef sirloin steak
Vegetable/Fruit:	3 medium green *or* red sweet peppers
	2 medium oranges

What a find! Cubes of marinated lamb or beef alternate on skewers with sweet peppers and orange wedges. (Pictured on page 16.)

For Marinade: In a medium mixing bowl combine all marinade ingredients.

To Prepare Meat: Trim fat from meat. Cut meat into 1-inch pieces. Place meat in a plastic bag set into a deep bowl. Pour marinade over meat in bag. Seal bag and turn meat to coat well. Marinate in the refrigerator for 6 to 24 hours, turning bag occasionally.

To Prepare Vegetable/Fruit: Remove seeds from peppers and cut peppers into 1½-inch pieces. Cut oranges into wedges.

To Prepare Kabobs: Remove meat pieces from bag, reserving marinade. On 6 long or 12 short metal skewers, alternately thread meat, pepper squares, and orange wedges, leaving about ¼ inch between pieces.

To Cook by Indirect Grill Method: In a covered grill arrange preheated coals around a drip pan. Test for *medium* heat above the pan. Place kabobs on the grill rack over the drip pan. Cover and grill for 16 to 18 minutes or till meat is desired doneness, brushing with reserved marinade halfway through grilling time.

To Cook by Direct Grill Method: Grill kabobs on the grill rack of an uncovered grill directly over *medium* coals for 12 to 14 minutes or till meat is desired doneness, turning once and brushing with reserved marinade halfway through grilling time.

Per serving: 311 calories / 18 g protein / 9 g carbohydrate / 22 g fat (7 g saturated) / 71 mg cholesterol / 112 mg sodium / 378 mg potassium.

Chicken Whirlibirds

Rotisserie or Indirect Grilling   Serves 12

Sauce:	¼	cup dry white wine
	2	tablespoons cooking oil
	2	tablespoons lemon juice
	1	tablespoon snipped parsley
	1	teaspoon dried rosemary, crushed
	1	teaspoon prepared mustard
	1	teaspoon Worcestershire sauce
	½	teaspoon salt
	¼	teaspoon celery seed
	¼	teaspoon pepper
Poultry:	2	2½- to 3-pound whole broiler-fryer chickens
Glaze:	¼	cup apple jelly

Twirl the birds on a spit or cook them on the rack of a covered grill.

For Sauce: In a small mixing bowl combine all sauce ingredients. Set aside.

To Prepare Poultry: Rinse chickens. Remove necks and giblets. Pat chickens dry. If desired, rub *salt* inside the body cavities. Skewer the neck skin to the back.

To Cook by Indirect Rotisserie Method: To mount one chicken on spit rod, place holding fork on rod, tines toward point; insert rod through chicken, pressing tines of holding fork firmly into breast meat. To tie wings, slip a 30-inch piece of string under back of chicken; bring ends of cord to front, looping around each wing tip. Tie in center of breast, leaving equal string ends. To tie legs, slip a 24-inch piece of string under tail. Loop string around tail, then around crossed legs. Tie very tightly to hold bird securely on spit, again leaving string ends. Pull together the strings attached to wings and legs; tie tightly.

Place the second chicken on spit rod so the tails of both birds meet. Secure with holding forks and tie as for first bird. Adjust holding forks and tighten screws. Test the balance.

In a covered grill arrange preheated coals around a drip pan. Test for *medium* heat where the birds will be. Attach spit, turn on the motor, and lower the grill hood. Let the birds rotate over the drip pan for 1¼ to 1¾ hours or till chicken is no longer pink and the drumsticks move easily, brushing every 15 minutes with sauce for the first 45 minutes.

Add jelly to remaining sauce; stir vigorously to remove all lumps of jelly. Brush jelly sauce onto chickens the last 15 to 30 minutes of grilling. Remove chickens from spit. Let stand, covered, for 15 minutes before carving.

To Cook by Indirect Grill Method: In a covered grill arrange preheated coals for indirect grilling. Test for *medium* heat where chickens will be. Place birds, breast side up, on a rack in a roasting pan. Place pan on grill rack, not directly over coals. Cover; grill for 1 to 1¼ hours or till chicken is no longer pink and drumsticks move easily, brushing every 15 minutes with sauce for first 45 minutes.

Add jelly to remaining sauce; stir well to remove all lumps. Brush jelly sauce onto chickens the last 15 to 30 minutes of grilling. Let stand, covered, 15 minutes before carving.

Per serving: 220 calories / 20 g protein / 5 g carbohydrate / 12 g fat (3 g saturated) / 65 mg cholesterol / 161 mg sodium / 185 mg potassium.

Chicken Whirlibirds

Chinese Smoked Ribs

Indirect Grilling   Serves 6

Sauce:	¼	cup catsup
	¼	cup soy sauce
	2	tablespoons brown sugar
	2	tablespoons water
	1	tablespoon grated gingerroot *or* 1 teaspoon ground ginger
Seasoning Rub:	2	tablespoons sugar
	½	teaspoon salt
	¼	teaspoon paprika
	¼	teaspoon ground turmeric
	¼	teaspoon celery seed
	¼	teaspoon dry mustard
Meat:	4	pounds pork loin back ribs or meaty spareribs
Wood Chips:	4	cups hickory *or* fruit wood chips

Fruit wood chips, such as apple, orange, and cherry, create a sweet smoky flavor that mingles pleasantly with the ginger. (Pictured on page 16.)

For Sauce: In a small mixing bowl combine all sauce ingredients. Cover and chill for up to 24 hours.

For Seasoning Rub: In a small mixing bowl combine all rub ingredients.

To Prepare Meat: Cut ribs into serving-size pieces. Rub seasoning mixture onto ribs. Cover and chill for 6 to 24 hours.

To Prepare Wood Chips: At least 1 hour before grilling, soak wood chips in enough water to cover. Drain chips.

To Cook by Indirect Grill Method: In a covered grill arrange preheated coals around a drip pan. Pour 1 inch of water into the drip pan. Sprinkle some of the drained wood chips onto the preheated coals. Test for *medium* heat above the pan. Place ribs on grill rack over the drip pan. Cover and grill for 1¼ to 1½ hours or till ribs are tender and no pink remains, adding more coals and wood chips as necessary and brushing the ribs with sauce the last 15 minutes of grilling.

Per serving: 519 calories / 35 g protein / 12 g carbohydrate / 36 g fat (14 g saturated) / 143 mg cholesterol / 1,094 mg sodium / 473 mg potassium.

Peanut-Buttered Pork Loin

Indirect Grilling   Makes 12 servings

Sauce:	⅓ cup orange juice
	¼ cup peanut butter
Meat:	1 3- to 5-pound boneless pork top loin roast (double loin tied)

One of America's favorite sandwich spreads combined with orange juice makes a winner of a sauce when brushed on this spectacular pork roast.

For Sauce: In a small mixing bowl gradually blend orange juice into peanut butter, beating with a wire whisk or fork till smooth. Set sauce aside.

To Prepare Meat: Trim fat from meat. Insert a meat thermometer near the center of roast.

To Cook by Indirect Grill Method: In a covered grill arrange preheated coals for indirect cooking. Test for *medium-low* heat where the meat will be. Place meat on a rack in a roasting pan on the grill rack. Cover and grill for 1¼ to 1¾ hours or till meat thermometer registers 140°. Brush roast with peanut butter sauce. Grill about 30 minutes more or till thermometer registers 160° to 170°, brushing occasionally with the sauce.

> **The '60s**
> When the neighbors dropped by, the rotisserie rose to the occasion. Whole birds, roasts, ribs, and legs of lamb twirled lazily over coals on rotating spits, while friends enjoyed the casual air of outdoor entertaining.

Per serving: 170 calories / 17 g protein / 2 g carbohydrate / 10 g fat (3 g saturated) / 51 mg cholesterol / 65 mg sodium / 256 mg potassium.

Burrito Burgers

Burrito Burgers

Indirect or Direct Grilling

Serves 8

Meat Mixture:	½ cup refried beans
	¼ cup chopped onion
	2 tablespoons chopped mild green chili peppers
	1½ pounds lean ground beef
	4 slices sharp American cheese (4 ounces), halved
Tortillas:	8 6- to 7-inch flour tortillas
Toppings:	2 cups chopped lettuce
	1 cup salsa *or* taco sauce
	1 small avocado, halved, seeded, peeled, and cut into thin slices

Olé! As Mexican foods gained popularity in the '70s, ingenious Americans seasoned their grilling with the flavors of Mexico. The results? A burger worth shouting about.

To Prepare Meat Mixture: In a medium mixing bowl combine all meat mixture ingredients *except* beef and cheese. Add ground beef and mix well. Shape mixture into eight patties (about 5 inches in diameter). Place a piece of cheese on one side of each patty. Fold meat over cheese, forming an oval; seal.

To Cook by Indirect Grill Method: In a covered grill arrange preheated coals around a drip pan. Test for *medium* heat above the pan. Place meat on the grill rack over the drip pan. Cover and grill for 20 to 24 minutes or till no pink remains.

To Cook by Direct Grill Method: Grill meat on the grill rack of an uncovered grill directly over *medium* coals for 14 to 18 minutes or till no pink remains, turning once halfway through grilling time.

For Tortillas: Meanwhile, wrap tortillas in foil and heat in a 350° oven for 10 minutes to soften. (*Or,* just before serving, place tortillas in a single layer on the grill rack for 1 minute.)

To Serve: Wrap heated tortillas around burgers. Serve with lettuce, salsa or taco sauce, and avocado slices.

Per serving: 311 calories / 18 g protein / 25 g carbohydrate / 16 g fat (6 g saturated) / 49 mg cholesterol / 446 mg sodium / 436 mg potassium.

Mock Gyros

Rotisserie or Indirect Grilling   Marinating Time: 6 to 24 hours   Serves 16

Marinade:	½	cup cooking oil
	½	cup lemon juice
	¼	cup finely chopped onion
	4	cloves garlic, minced
Meat:	1	5- to 6-pound leg of lamb, boned and butterflied
	1	2-pound boneless beef round steak
	1	tablespoon salt
	2	teaspoons dried thyme, crushed
	2	teaspoons ground coriander
	1	teaspoon pepper
Sauce:	1	8-ounce carton plain yogurt
	½	cup chopped cucumber
	1	clove garlic, minced
Bread:	16	large pita bread rounds, halved crosswise
Toppings:	2	medium tomatoes, chopped
	1	cup snipped parsley

A recipe that's fit for a crowd—gather your neighbors and invite them in to indulge in these gyro-style sandwiches with authentic Greek flavor.

For Marinade: In a small mixing bowl combine all marinade ingredients. Set aside.

To Prepare Meat: Place lamb, cut side up, and beef side by side; cover with plastic wrap. Pound each piece of meat to a 16x12-inch rectangle, ½ to ¾ inch thick. Cut and patch meats where necessary to make the surface even.

Combine salt, thyme, coriander, and pepper; sprinkle over meat. Pound in seasonings. Place beef atop lamb; pound together. Fold meat; place in a plastic bag set into a shallow dish. Pour marinade over meat. Seal bag and turn meat. Marinate in the refrigerator 6 to 24 hours; turn occasionally.

Remove meat from bag; reserve and chill marinade. Unfold meat and roll up jelly-roll style, beginning at narrow end. Tie meat at 1½ to 2 inch intervals. Tie lengthwise. Tie once more between each crosswise string and 1 inch from each end.

To Cook by Indirect Rotisserie Method: Insert spit rod lenthwise through the meat, centering the meat on the spit and securing with holding forks. Test the balance. Arrange preheated coals around a drip pan; test for *medium* heat where the meat will be. Attach spit, turn on the motor, and lower the grill hood. Let meat rotate over drip pan for 1½ to 2 hours or till rare to medium-rare (140° to 150°), brushing occasionally with reserved marinade during the first 45 minutes. Remove meat from spit.

To Cook by Indirect Grill Method: In a covered grill arrange preheated coals for indirect grilling. Test for *medium* heat where meat will be. Place meat on a rack in a roasting pan on the grill rack, not directly over coals. Cover and grill for 1½ to 2 hours or till rare to medium-rare (140° to 150°), brushing occasionally with the reserved marinade during the first 45 minutes.

To Serve: Combine all sauce ingredients. Thinly slice meat crosswise, removing strings as you slice. Serve meat with pita bread. Top with yogurt sauce, tomatoes, and parsley.

Per serving: 475 calories / 39 g protein / 24 g carbohydrate / 24 g fat (8 g saturated) / 112 mg cholesterol / 708 mg sodium / 606 mg potassium.

Mock Gyros

Cheese-Topped Tomatoes
(see recipe, page 29)

Garlic-Buttered Shrimp
(see recipe, page 28)

Garlic-Buttered Shrimp

Indirect Grilling   Serves 4

Seafood:	1	pound fresh *or* frozen large shrimp in shells (about 20) (thawed, if frozen)
Sauce:	2	tablespoons margarine *or* butter
	2	cloves garlic, minced
	1	tablespoon snipped parsley
		Dash ground red pepper
	3	tablespoons dry white wine

Busy cooks will savor this delightfully easy scampi-style shrimp. (Pictured on page 27.)

To Prepare Seafood: Peel and devein shrimp, keeping tails intact.

For Sauce: In a small saucepan melt margarine or butter. Stir in garlic, parsley, and red pepper; cook about 1 minute. Stir in wine; heat through. Set sauce aside.

To Prepare Kabobs: Thread shrimp onto 4 long or 8 short metal skewers, leaving about ¼ inch between each.

To Cook by Indirect Grill Method: In a covered grill arrange preheated coals around a drip pan. Test for *medium* heat above the pan. Place kabobs on the grill rack over the drip pan. Cover and grill for 4 to 6 minutes or till shrimp turn opaque, turning often and brushing frequently with sauce.

To Serve: If desired, serve shrimp on a bed of shredded lettuce.

Per serving: 146 calories / 14 g protein / 3 g carbohydrate / 8 g fat (1 g saturated) / 132 mg cholesterol / 232 mg sodium / 148 mg potassium.

Cheese-Topped Tomatoes

Direct Grilling   Serves 4

Topping:	½ cup soft bread crumbs (about ½ slice)
	½ cup shredded sharp American cheese (2 ounces)
	1 tablespoon margarine *or* butter, melted
Vegetable:	2 large tomatoes
	1 tablespoon snipped parsley *or* desired fresh herb

From garden to grill—vine-ripened tomatoes topped with cheese make for a sumptuous side dish. (Pictured on page 27.)

For Topping: In a small mixing bowl combine all topping ingredients. Set aside.

To Prepare Vegetable: Slice tomatoes in half, using a sawtooth cut, if desired. Sprinkle with *salt* and *pepper*. Then sprinkle tomatoes with topping and parsley or herb. Tear off an 18x18-inch piece of heavy foil. Place tomatoes in the center of the foil. Bring up two opposite edges of foil and seal with a double fold. Then fold remaining ends to completely enclose the tomatoes, leaving space for steam to build.

To Cook by Direct Grill Method: Grill foil packet, seam side up, on the grill rack of an uncovered grill directly over *medium* or *medium-hot* coals about 20 minutes or till heated through. Serve immediately.

The '70s
Equal rights commanded front-page headlines in the 1970s as record numbers of women joined the work force. Although Mom's schedule became even more demanding than before, the second income enabled families to afford extras. For two-career households, streamlined barbecue menus and a proliferation of convenience foods made outdoor grilling easier than ever.

Per serving: 118 calories / 5 g protein / 8 g carbohydrate / 8 g fat (3 g saturated) / 13 mg cholesterol / 276 mg sodium / 288 mg potassium.

Texas-Style Beef Brisket with Five-Alarm Sauce

Indirect Grilling   Serves 12

Wood Chips:	4 to 6 cups mesquite wood chips
Brushing Sauce:	¼ cup dry red wine
	4 teaspoons Worcestershire sauce
	1 tablespoon cooking oil
	1 tablespoon red wine *or* cider vinegar
	1 clove garlic, minced
	½ crushed coriander seed
	½ teaspoon hot-style mustard
	Dash ground red pepper
Seasoning Rub:	2 teaspoons seasoned salt
	1 teaspoon paprika
	1 teaspoon pepper
Meat:	1 2- to 3-pound fresh beef brisket
Sauce:	5-Alarm Sauce*

Texas barbecue means cooking beef ever-so-slowly over mesquite wood chips and slathering it with two kinds of sauce—a tangy, spiced brush-on and a fiery, sweet red sauce.

To Prepare Wood Chips: At least 1 hour before grilling, soak wood chips in enough water to cover. Drain chips.

For Brushing Sauce: In a small mixing bowl combine all brushing sauce ingredients. Set aside.

For Seasoning Rub: In a small mixing bowl combine all seasoning rub ingredients.

To Prepare Meat: Trim excess fat from brisket. Rub seasoning mixture onto meat.

To Cook by Indirect Grill Method: In a covered grill arrange preheated coals around a drip pan. Pour 1 inch of water into the drip pan. Sprinkle some of the drained wood chips onto the preheated coals. Test for *slow* heat above the pan. Place brisket, fat side up, on the grill rack over the drip pan. Cover and grill for 2 to 2½ hours or till meat is very tender. Every 30 minutes or as needed, brush meat with brushing sauce and add more coals, drained wood chips, and water for the drip pan.

To Serve: Thinly slice meat across the grain. Arrange meat on plates and top with some of the 5-Alarm Sauce. Pass the remaining sauce.

***5-Alarm Sauce:** In a small saucepan stir together 1 cup *catsup*; 1 large *tomato*, peeled, seeded, and chopped (¾ cup); 1 small *green sweet pepper*, chopped (½ cup); 2 tablespoons chopped *onion*; 2 tablespoons *brown sugar*; 1 to 2 tablespoons *steak sauce*; 1 to 2 tablespoons *Worcestershire sauce*; ½ teaspoon *garlic powder*; ¼ teaspoon *ground nutmeg*; ¼ teaspoon *ground cinnamon*; ¼ teaspoon *ground cloves*; ⅛ teaspoon *ground ginger*; and ⅛ teaspoon *pepper*. Bring to boiling; reduce heat. Cover and simmer about 5 minutes or till green pepper is crisp-tender. Serve warm or at room temperature. Makes about 2½ cups.

Per serving: 192 calories / 17 g protein / 11 g carbohydrate / 9 g fat (3 g saturated) / 52 mg cholesterol / 546 mg sodium / 364 mg potassium.

Moroccan-Style Lamb Chops
(see recipe, page 32)

Texas-Style Beef Brisket

Fiesta Grilled Peppers *(see recipe, page 33)*

Moroccan-Style Lamb Chops

Indirect or Direct Grilling	Marinating Time: 6 to 24 hours	Serves 4

Marinade:	¾	cup plain yogurt
	3	tablespoons orange juice
	2	tablespoons sliced green onion
	1½	teaspoons ground coriander
	½	teaspoon salt
	½	teaspoon ground cumin
	½	teaspoon ground cardamom
	¼	teaspoon ground cinnamon
	¼	teaspoon ground cloves
	¼	teaspoon ground ginger
Sauce:	1	medium cucumber, chopped (1¼ cups)
	1	medium tomato, chopped (⅔ cup)
	½	cup chopped onion (1 medium)
	½	cup plain yogurt
	⅛	teaspoon salt
Meat:	8	lamb loin chops, cut 1 inch thick (4 to 5 ounces each)
Accompaniment:		Hot cooked couscous or rice (optional)
Garnish:		Cilantro (optional)

Marinate lamb chops overnight in a spicy yogurt sauce for a quick-grilling entrée the next day.

For Marinade: In a small mixing bowl combine all marinade ingredients. Set aside.

For Sauce: In a mixing bowl combine all sauce ingredients. Cover and chill sauce till serving time.

To Prepare Meat: Arrange lamb chops in a shallow dish. Pour marinade over chops, turning to coat. Cover and marinate in the refrigerator for 6 to 24 hours. Remove chops from marinade, reserving as much marinade as possible.

To Cook by Indirect Grill Method: In a covered grill arrange preheated coals around a drip pan. Test for *medium* heat above the pan. Place lamb chops on the grill rack over the drip pan. Cover and grill for 16 to 18 minutes (for rare; 18 to 20 minutes for medium) or till desired doneness, brushing with reserved marinade halfway through grilling time.

To Cook by Direct Grill Method: Grill lamb chops on the grill rack of an uncovered grill directly over *medium* coals for 14 to 16 minutes or till desired doneness, turning chops once and brushing with reserved marinade halfway through grilling time.

To Serve: Arrange chops on dinner plates. If desired, serve with couscous or rice and garnish each serving with cilantro. Pass sauce.

Per serving: 332 calories / 39 g protein / 12 g carbohydrate / 14 g fat (5 g saturated) / 115 mg cholesterol / 473 mg sodium / 713 mg potassium.

Fiesta Grilled Peppers

Direct Grilling   Serves 12

Vegetable:	8 to 10 green, yellow, *and/or* red sweet peppers
	2 to 3 tablespoons olive oil *or* cooking oil

Visit your local farmers' market to find brightly colored peppers at a reasonable price. (Pictured on page 31.)

To Prepare Vegetable: Cut the peppers into quarters. Remove stem ends, seeds, and membranes. Brush skins with oil.

To Cook by Direct Grill Method: Lay peppers, skin side down, perpendicular to wires on grill rack so peppers don't fall into coals. Grill peppers on the grill rack of an uncovered grill directly over *medium-low* coals about 15 minutes or till crisp-tender and lightly charred.

The '80s and into the '90s

Barbecue moved down home and uptown all at once in the '80s. Baby boomers rediscovered barbecue's roots in such foods as Texas-Style Beef Brisket (see recipe, page 30). Meanwhile, urbanites flocked to upbeat eateries, where mesquite grilling and blackened redfish were the rage.

As in the '50s, families today are centering their lives around their homes. But with Mom and Dad both working, families are busier than ever. To keep pace with on-the-go lifestyles, meals must be quick and easy, as well as flavorful, fresh, and nutritious. That means lots of recipes for fast-grilling cuts of poultry, fish, and lean meats, plus generous portions of fresh fruits and vegetables.

Per serving: 33 calories / 0 g protein / 3 g carbohydrate / 2 g fat (0 g saturated) / 0 mg cholesterol / 1 mg sodium / 81 mg potassium.

Lamb with Herb-Dijon Sauce

Indirect Grilling   Marinating Time: 6 to 24 hours   Serves 12

Marinade:	1	8-ounce jar (¾ cup) Dijon-style mustard
	⅓	cup dry white wine
	¼	cup cooking oil
	2	cloves garlic, minced
	1	teaspoon dried rosemary, crushed
	1	teaspoon dried basil, crushed
	½	teaspoon dried oregano, crushed
	½	teaspoon dried thyme, crushed
	¼	teaspoon pepper
Meat:	1	5- to 6-pound leg of lamb

For a tasty alternative, serve this zippy mustard sauce over beef, pork, or chicken.

For Marinade: In a small mixing bowl combine all marinade ingredients.

To Prepare Meat: Have your butcher bone and butterfly the leg of lamb. Place lamb in shall dish. Spread lamb with marinade mixture. Cover and marinate for 6 to 24 hours in the refrigerator.

Drain meat, reserving the marinade. Thread two 12- to 14-inch metal skewers diagonally through the meat to keep it flat during grilling.

To Cook by Indirect Grill Method: In a covered grill arrange preheated coals around a drip pan. Test for *medium-low* heat above the pan. Place meat on the grill rack over the drip pan. Cover and grill for 1 to 1½ hours or till slightly pink in center, brushing meat with the reserved marinade during the first 45 minutes of grilling.

To Serve: In a small saucepan bring remaining marinade to boiling. Boil for 1 minute, stirring constantly. Pass heated mixture with meat.

Per serving: 348 calories / 29 g protein / 2 g carbohydrate / 24 g fat (8 g saturated) / 100 mg cholesterol / 547 mg sodium / 379 mg potassium.

BIRDS OF A FEATHER

■

With today's emphasis on healthful eating, chicken,

turkey, and Cornish hens have become popular choices

for grilling. Poultry is so versatile, that no matter

whether you marinate it, sauce it, spice it, herb it,

stuff it, or skewer it, you can't lose!

Fresh Garden Chicken

Indirect or Direct Grilling   Serves 4

Brushing Sauce:	½	cup salsa
	1	tablespoon lime juice
Poultry:	1	2½- to 3-pound broiler-fryer chicken, quartered
Vegetable Sauce:	½	cup mild salsa
	½	cup finely chopped cucumber
	¼	cup chopped green pepper
	1	tablespoon snipped cilantro
	1	tablespoon lime juice

Cilantro, also known as Chinese parsley, gives a distictively fresh flavor to Mexican and other Latin American dishes. If you don't have fresh cilantro on hand, use fresh parsley.

For Brushing Sauce: In a small mixing bowl combine all brushing sauce ingredients. Set sauce aside.

To Prepare Poultry: If desired, remove skin from chicken. Rinse chicken; pat dry. Sprinkle with *salt* and *pepper*.

To Cook by Indirect Grill Method: In a covered grill arrange preheated coals around a drip pan. Test for *medium* heat above the pan. Place chicken, bone side down, on the grill rack over the drip pan. Cover and grill for 50 to 60 minutes or till chicken is tender and no longer pink, brushing frequently with brushing sauce the last 10 minutes of grilling.

To Cook by Direct Grill Method: Place chicken, bone side up, on the grill rack of an uncovered grill. Grill directly over *medium* coals for 40 to 50 minutes or till chicken is tender and no longer pink, turning once halfway through grilling time and brushing frequently with brushing sauce the last 10 minutes of grilling.

For Vegetable Sauce: In a small saucepan combine all vegetable sauce ingredients. Bring just to boiling. Remove from heat; keep warm. Spoon vegetable sauce over chicken.

Per serving: 292 calories / 31 g protein / 6 g carbohydrate / 17 g fat (4 g saturated) / 98 mg cholesterol / 448 mg sodium / 463 mg potassium.

Fresh Garden Chicken

Peanut-Ginger Chicken with California Salsa

Indirect Grilling	Marinating Time: 6 to 24 hours	Serves 6

Marinade:	½ cup hot water
	½ cup creamy peanut butter
	¼ cup chili sauce
	¼ cup soy sauce
	2 tablespoons salad oil
	2 tablespoons vinegar
	4 cloves garlic, minced
	2 teaspoons grated gingerroot *or* ½ teaspoon ground ginger
	¼ teaspoon ground red pepper
Poultry:	12 chicken thighs (about 3 pounds)
Salsa:	1 cup chopped fresh fruit (such as peeled peaches, nectarines, pears, *or* plums)
	1 cup chopped, seeded cucumber
	1 green onion, thinly sliced (2 tablespoons)
	2 tablespoons snipped parsley *or* cilantro
	1 tablespoon sugar
	1 tablespoon salad oil
	1 tablespoon vinegar

To let this spicy peanut butter marinade really soak in, bathe these tender, juicy chicken pieces in it overnight.

For Marinade: In a small mixing bowl gradually stir hot water into peanut butter. (The mixture will stiffen at first.) Stir in remaining marinade ingredients.

To Prepare Poultry: Remove skin from chicken. Rinse chicken; pat dry. Place chicken in a plastic bag set into a deep bowl. Pour marinade over chicken in bag. Seal bag and turn chicken to coat well. Marinate in the refrigerator for 6 to 24 hours, turning bag occasionally. Remove chicken from bag; discard marinade.

For Salsa: In a medium mixing bowl combine all salsa ingredients. Cover and chill for 1 to 2 hours.

To Cook by Indirect Grill Method: In a covered grill arrange preheated coals around a drip pan. Test for *medium* heat above the pan. Place chicken, bone side down, on the grill rack over the drip pan. Cover and grill for 35 to 45 minutes or till chicken is tender and no longer pink. Spoon some salsa over chicken; pass the remaining salsa.

Per serving: 272 calories / 27 g protein / 7 g carbohydrate / 15 g fat (4 g saturated) / 93 mg cholesterol / 203 mg sodium / 357 mg potassium.

Tandoori Chicken

	Indirect Grilling	Marinating Time: 6 to 24 hours	Serves 4

Marinade:	1	8-ounce carton plain yogurt
	2	tablespoons lemon juice
	2	teaspoons grated gingerroot *or* ¾ teaspoon ground ginger
	1	teaspoon ground coriander
	½	teaspoon ground cumin
	¼	teaspoon ground turmeric
	⅛	teaspoon ground red pepper
	1	clove garlic, minced
Poultry:	4	whole chicken breasts (about 1½ pounds total), halved lengthwise

In India, this popular poultry dish is cooked in special ovens called tandoors. Your backyard grill and a spicy yogurt marinade replicate the traditional flavor.

For Marinade: In a small mixing bowl combine all marinade ingredients.

To Prepare Poultry: If desired, remove skin from chicken. Rinse chicken; pat dry. Place chicken in a plastic bag set into a deep bowl. Pour marinade over chicken in bag. Seal bag and turn chicken to coat well. Marinate in the refrigerator for 6 to 24 hours, turning bag occasionally. Remove chicken from bag, reserving marinade. Chill reserved marinade while grilling chicken.

To Cook by Indirect Grill Method: In a covered grill arrange preheated coals around a drip pan. Test for *medium* heat above the pan. Place chicken, bone side down, on the grill rack over the drip pan. Cover and grill for 50 to 60 minutes or till chicken is tender and no longer pink, brushing with marinade the last 10 minutes of grilling.

Per serving: 224 calories / 31 g protein / 6 g carbohydrate / 8 g fat (3 g saturated) / 81 mg cholesterol / 106 mg sodium / 390 mg potassium.

Sizzling Sesame Chicken with Vegetables

Indirect or Direct Grilling   Serves 4

Sauce:	½ cup chicken broth
	3 tablespoons soy sauce
	1 teaspoon cornstarch
	2 teaspoons toasted sesame oil
	1 teaspoon sugar
	1 clove garlic, minced
	1 tablespoon sesame seed
Poultry:	2 pounds meaty chicken pieces (breasts, thighs, and drumsticks)
Vegetables:	1 large red or green sweet pepper, cut into 1-inch strips
	1 medium zucchini, halved crosswise and cut into 3x1-inch strips

Grilled red pepper and zucchini strips complement the sesame flavor of this Oriental-style chicken.

For Sauce: In a small saucepan combine all sauce ingredients *except* sesame seed. Cook and stir till thickened and bubbly. Cook and stir for 2 minutes more. Stir in sesame seed. Remove from heat; set aside.

To Prepare Poultry: If desired, remove skin from chicken. Rinse chicken; pat dry.

To Cook by Indirect Grill Method: In a covered grill arrange preheated coals around a drip pan. Test for *medium* heat above the pan. Place chicken, bone side down, on the grill rack over the drip pan. Cover and grill for 50 to 60 minutes or till chicken is tender and no longer pink, brushing frequently with sauce the last 10 minutes of grilling. Place the pepper and zucchini beside the chicken perpendicular to the wires on the grill rack for the last 15 minutes of grilling, brushing occasionally with sauce.

To Cook by Direct Grill Method: Place chicken, bone side up, on the grill rack of an uncovered grill. Grill directly over *medium* coals for 35 to 45 minutes or till chicken is tender and no longer pink, turning once halfway through grilling time and brushing frequently with sauce the last 10 minutes of grilling. Place the pepper and zucchini beside the chicken perpendicular to the wires on the grill rack for the last 10 minutes of grilling, brushing occasionally with sauce.

Per serving: 308 calories / 35 g protein / 5 g carbohydrate / 16 g fat (4 g saturated) / 104 mg cholesterol / 961 mg sodium / 426 mg potassium.

Curried Chicken

Indirect or Direct Grilling   Serves 4

Sauce:	3 tablespoons honey
	2 tablespoons dry white wine *or* white wine vinegar
	2 teaspoons curry powder
	½ teaspoon garlic salt
	¼ teaspoon paprika
	Dash ground red pepper
Poultry:	2 pounds meaty chicken pieces (breasts, thighs, and drumsticks)

A spicy sweet sauce perks up grilled chicken pieces.

For Sauce: In a small mixing bowl combine all sauce ingredients. Set aside.

To Prepare Poultry: If desired, remove skin from chicken. Rinse chicken; pat dry.

To Cook by Indirect Grill Method: In a covered grill arrange preheated coals around a drip pan. Test for *medium* heat above the pan. Place chicken, bone side down, on the grill rack over the drip pan. Cover and grill for 50 to 60 minutes or till chicken is tender and no longer pink, brushing frequently with sauce the last 10 minutes of grilling.

To Cook by Direct Grill Method: Place chicken, bone side up, on the grill rack of an uncovered grill. Grill directly over *medium* coals for 35 to 45 minutes or till chicken is tender and no longer pink, turning once halfway through grilling time and brushing frequently with sauce during the last 10 minutes of grilling.

Per serving: 308 calories / 33 g protein / 14 g carbohydrate / 13 g fat (3 g saturated) / 104 mg cholesterol / 307 mg sodium / 310 mg potassium.

Spicy Thai Chicken

Spicy Thai Chicken

Indirect or Direct Grilling   Serves 4

Sauce:		
	1	8-ounce can tomatoes
	¼	cup raisins
	2	tablespoons currant jelly
	1	tablespoon canned chopped green chili peppers
	1	clove garlic
	2	teaspoons vinegar
	¼ to ½	teaspoon crushed red pepper
		Dash salt
Poultry:	1	2½- to 3-pound broiler-fryer chicken, cut up

Raisins and currant jelly sweeten the tangy tomato sauce.

For Sauce: In a blender container or food processor bowl combine all sauce ingredients. Cover and blend or process till smooth. Transfer to a small saucepan. Bring to boiling; reduce heat. Simmer, uncovered, about 10 minutes or till sauce reaches brushing consistency. Remove from heat; set aside.

To Prepare Poultry: If desired, remove skin from chicken. Rinse chicken; pat dry.

To Cook by Indirect Grill Method: In a covered grill arrange preheated coals around a drip pan. Test for *medium* heat above the pan. Place chicken, bone side down, on the grill rack over the drip pan. Cover and grill for 50 to 60 minutes or till chicken is tender and no longer pink, brushing frequently with sauce the last 10 minutes of grilling.

To Cook by Direct Grill Method: Place chicken, bone side up, on the grill rack of an uncovered grill. Grill directly over *medium* coals for 35 to 45 minutes or till chicken is tender and no longer pink, turning once halfway through grilling time and brushing frequently with sauce during the last 10 minutes of grilling.

Per serving: 332 calories / 31 g protein / 17 g carbohydrate / 15 g fat (4 g saturated) / 98 mg cholesterol / 250 mg sodium / 466 mg potassium.

Orange-Glazed Chicken

Indirect or Direct Grilling   Serves 4

Glaze:	⅓	cup frozen orange juice concentrate, thawed
	¼	cup honey
	¼	cup soy sauce
	1	teaspoon five-spice powder
	½	teaspoon garlic powder
Poultry:	2	pounds meaty chicken pieces (breasts, thighs, and drumsticks)
Garnish:	1	small orange

Soy sauce and five-spice powder add a touch of the Orient to this honey-and-orange sauced chicken.

For Glaze: In a small mixing bowl combine all glaze ingredients. Set aside.

To Prepare Poultry: If desired, remove skin from chicken. Rinse chicken; pat dry.

To Cook by Indirect Grill Method: In a covered grill arrange preheated coals around a drip pan. Test for *medium* heat above the pan. Place chicken, bone side down, on the grill rack over the drip pan. Cover and grill for 50 to 60 minutes or till chicken is tender and no longer pink, brushing occasionally with glaze the last 10 minutes of grilling.

To Cook by Direct Grill Method: Place chicken, bone side up, on the grill rack of an uncovered grill. Grill directly over *medium* coals for 35 to 45 minutes or till chicken is tender and no longer pink, turning once halfway through grilling time and brushing occasionally with glaze during the last 10 minutes of grilling.

To Serve: Cut the orange into thin slices. Garnish chicken with orange slices.

The Smoke-Cooking Secret

Add some pizzazz to ordinary steak, ribs, chicken, and fish by discovering the satisfying outdoor, smoky flavor that wood chips and chunks can add. Start with one type of wood, then experiment with combinations of different woods. Just keep in mind the flavor produced by the wood should blend with the flavor of the food you're grilling.

Hickory, an ever-so-popular wood, will add an intense, sweet flavor to barbecued foods.

For a light, sweet, smoky flavor, try mesquite. It is also available in a charcoal briquette form.

When you prefer a delicately sweet smoke, try using apple, cherry, or Osage orange wood.

Be sure to use only those woods from either fruit or nut trees. Soft woods, such as pine, should not be used because their resins discolor the food and give it a bitter taste.

Once you'ved decided on the type of wood chips or chunks to use, soak them in enough water to cover for at least 1 hour, then drain. (If indirect grilling, add an inch of water to the drip pan.) Sprinkle the chips or chunks on the hot coals. Add more chips or chunks every 15 to 20 minutes and more water to the drip pan as necessary.

Per serving: 387 calories / 35 g protein / 33 g carbohydrate / 13 g fat (3 g saturated) / 104 mg cholesterol / 1,123 mg sodium / 570 mg potassium.

Marinated Chicken Breasts with Mushroom Sauce

Indirect or Direct Grilling	Marinating Time: 6 to 24 hours	Serves 4

Marinade:	½ cup dry white wine
	2 tablespoons olive oil *or* cooking oil
	1 teaspoon dried oregano, crushed
	1 teaspoon dried basil, crushed
	2 cloves garlic, minced
Poultry:	2 whole medium chicken breasts (about 1½ pounds), skinned and halved lengthwise
Sauce:	1 cup sliced fresh mushrooms
	1 tablespoon margarine *or* butter
	¼ cup dry white wine
Accompaniment:	2 cups hot cooked rice *or* couscous

For this elegant chicken dinner, the breasts are marinated in white wine and herbs, grilled till tender, and then served smothered in mushrooms.

For Marinade: In a small mixing bowl combine all marinade ingredients.

To Prepare Poultry: Rinse chicken; pat dry. Place chicken in a plastic bag set into a deep bowl. Pour marinade over chicken in bag. Seal bag and turn chicken to coat well. Marinate in the refrigerator for 6 to 24 hours, turning bag occasionally. Remove chicken from bag, reserving marinade. Chill reserved marinade while grilling chicken.

To Cook by Indirect Grill Method: In a covered grill arrange preheated coals around a drip pan. Test for *medium* heat above the pan. Place chicken, bone side down, on the grill rack over the drip pan. Cover and grill for 50 to 60 minutes or till chicken is tender and no longer pink, brushing occasionally with reserved marinade during the first 35 minutes.

To Cook by Direct Grill Method: Place chicken, bone side up, on the grill rack of an uncovered grill. Grill directly over *medium* coals for 35 to 45 minutes or till chicken is tender and no longer pink, brushing occasionally with reserved marinade during the first 20 minutes and turning once.

For Sauce: In a small saucepan cook mushrooms in margarine or butter till tender. Stir in wine. Bring to boiling; reduce heat. Simmer, uncovered, for 5 minutes.

To Serve: Place chicken breasts on rice or couscous. Spoon sauce over the chicken.

Per serving: 193 calories / 21 g protein / 2 g carbohydrate / 9 g fat (2 g saturated) / 57 mg cholesterol / 86 mg sodium / 274 mg potassium.

Grilled German Potato Salad
(see recipe, page 171)

Zesty Drumsticks

Zesty Drumsticks

Indirect or Direct Grilling   Serves 4

Sauce:	¼ cup currant jelly
	¼ cup chili sauce
	1 tablespoon vinegar
	1 tablespoon Worcestershire sauce
	⅛ teaspoon garlic powder
	Several drops bottled hot pepper sauce
Poultry:	8 chicken drumsticks (about 1½ pounds)

These brightly sauced chicken legs will be enjoyed by the whole family. For an added bonus, you can eat them with your fingers.

For Sauce: In a small saucepan combine all sauce ingredients. Cook over low heat about 5 minutes or till bubbly, stirring occasionally to melt jelly. Remove from heat; set aside.

To Prepare Poultry: If desired, remove skin from chicken. Rinse chicken; pat dry.

To Cook by Indirect Grill Method: In a covered grill arrange preheated coals around a drip pan. Test for *medium* heat above the pan. Place chicken on the grill rack over the drip pan. Cover and grill for 50 to 60 minutes or till chicken is tender and no longer pink, brushing frequently with sauce the last 10 minutes of grilling.

To Cook by Direct Grill Method: Place chicken on the grill rack of an uncovered grill. Grill directly over *medium* coals for 35 to 45 minutes or till chicken is tender and no longer pink, turning once halfway through grilling time and brushing frequently with sauce the last 10 minutes of grilling.

Per serving: 196 calories / 21 g protein / 18 g carbohydrate / 4 g fat (1 g saturated) / 69 mg cholesterol / 311 mg sodium / 286 mg potassium.

Herbed-Mustard Chicken Quarters

Indirect or Direct Grilling   Serves 4

Sauce:		
	1	tablespoon snipped parsley
	1	tablespoon water
	1	tablespoon mayonnaise *or* salad dressing
	1	tablespoon Dijon-style mustard
	1	teaspoon dried oregano, crushed
	⅛	teaspoon ground red pepper
Poultry:	1	2½- to 3-pound broiler-fryer chicken, cut into quarters

Another time, brush this oregano-scented sauce on pork chops.

For Sauce: In a small bowl combine all sauce ingredients. Cover and refrigerate sauce till ready to use.

To Prepare Poultry: If desired, remove skin from chicken. Rinse chicken; pat dry.

To Cook by Indirect Grill Method: In a covered grill arrange preheated coals around a drip pan. Test for *medium* heat above the pan. Place chicken, bone side down, on the grill rack over the drip pan. Cover and grill for 50 to 60 minutes or till chicken is tender and no longer pink, brushing occasionally with sauce the last 10 minutes of grilling.

To Cook by Direct Grill Method: Place chicken, bone side up, on the grill rack of an uncovered grill. Grill directly over *medium* coals for 40 to 50 minutes or till chicken is tender and no longer pink, turning once halfway through grilling time and brushing occasionally with sauce during the last 10 minutes of grilling.

Per serving: 297 calories / 31 g protein / 1 g carbohydrate / 18 g fat (5 g saturated) / 100 mg cholesterol / 206 mg sodium / 265 mg potassium.

Grilled Chicken with Apricot and Brown Rice Pilaf

Indirect or Direct Grilling   Serves 4

Accompaniment:	Apricot and Brown Rice Pilaf (see recipe, page 172)
Sauce:	3 tablespoons lemon juice
	2 tablespoons olive oil *or* cooking oil
	½ teaspoon dried thyme, crushed
	¼ teaspoon finely shredded lemon peel
Poultry:	2 to 2½ pounds meaty chicken pieces (breasts, thighs, and drumsticks)

Choose a fruity olive oil to enhance the simple lemon basting sauce.

To Prepare Accompaniment: Prepare Apricot and Brown Rice Pilaf. Place in packet according to directions. Set aside.

For Sauce: In a small mixing bowl combine all sauce ingredients. Set aside.

To Prepare Poultry: If desired, remove skin from chicken. Rinse chicken; pat dry.

To Cook by Indirect Grill Method: In a covered grill arrange preheated coals around a drip pan. Test for *medium* heat above the pan. Place chicken, bone side down, on the grill rack over the drip pan. Cover and grill for 50 to 60 minutes or till chicken is tender and no longer pink, brushing frequently with sauce the last 10 minutes of grilling. Place the foil packet of pilaf beside the chicken on the grill rack. Grill foil packet directly over *medium-high* coals the last 15 minutes of grilling. Fluff rice with a fork before serving.

To Cook by Direct Grill Method: Place chicken, bone side up, on the grill rack of an uncovered grill. Grill directly over *medium* coals for 35 to 45 minutes or till chicken is tender and no longer pink, turning once halfway through grilling time and brushing frequently with sauce the last 10 minutes of grilling. Place the foil packet of pilaf beside the chicken on the grill rack. Grill foil packet directly over *medium* coals during the last 20 minutes of grilling. Fluff rice with a fork before serving.

Per serving: 314 calories / 33 g protein / 1 g carbohydrate / 19 g fat (4 g saturated) / 104 mg cholesterol / 92 mg sodium / 292 mg potassium.

Grilled Cajun Chicken Salad

Indirect or Direct Grilling   Serves 4

Dressing:	¼	cup salad oil
	¼	cup vinegar
	1	tablespoon sugar
	1	tablespoon snipped fresh thyme *or* ½ teaspoon dried thyme, crushed
	¼	teaspoon dry mustard
Sauce:	1	tablespoon salad oil
	1	teaspoon onion powder
	½	teaspoon pepper
	¼	teaspoon ground red pepper
	¼	teaspoon salt
Poultry:	4	skinless, boneless chicken breast halves (about 1 pound total)
Vegetables:	4	cups torn mixed greens
	1	medium carrot, shredded
	¼	cup sliced and halved radishes
	1	green onion, sliced (2 tablespoons)

Toss bits of peppery chicken with fresh-from-the-garden greens and vegetables.

For Dressing: In a screw-top jar combine all dressing ingredients. Cover and shake well. Chill till serving time.

For Sauce: In a small mixing bowl combine all sauce ingredients. Set aside.

To Prepare Poultry: Rinse chicken; pat dry.

To Cook by Indirect Grill Method: In a covered grill arrange preheated coals around a drip pan. Test for *medium* heat above the pan. Place chicken on the grill rack over the drip pan. Brush with *half* of the sauce. Cover and grill for 15 to 18 minutes or till chicken is tender and no longer pink, brushing occaionally with remaining sauce.

To Cook by Direct Grill Method: Place chicken on the grill rack of an uncovered grill. Brush with *half* of the sauce. Grill directly over *medium* coals for 12 to 15 minutes or till chicken is tender and no longer pink, turning once and brushing occasionally with remaining sauce.

To Serve: In a large salad bowl combine all vegetable ingredients. Cut chicken into bite-size pieces. Add chicken and dressing to salad. Toss to mix.

Per serving: 305 calories / 23 g protein / 8 g carbohydrate / 20 g fat (3 g saturated) / 59 mg cholesterol / 219 mg sodium / 471 mg potassium.

Grilled Cajun Chicken Salad

Chicken Pinwheels

Indirect or Direct Grilling		Serves 4
Poultry:	4 skinless, boneless chicken breast halves (about 1 pound total)	
	2 to 3 ounces thinly sliced prosciutto *or* very thinly sliced ham	
Sauce:	2 tablespoons margarine *or* butter, melted	
	1 tablespoon lemon juice	
	½ teaspoon dried thyme, crushed	
	¼ teaspoon garlic powder	

Welcome spring with these succulent chicken breasts. Serve them with steamed asparagus and pasta tossed with butter and Parmesan cheese.

To Prepare Poultry: Rinse chicken; pat dry. Cut chicken into ½-inch-wide strips. Cut prosciutto into ½-inch-wide strips. Divide chicken and prosciutto strips into 4 portions. Place a strip of prosciutto on each strip of chicken. For each serving, form one strip into a pinwheel with prosciutto inside. Add remaining strips, one at a time, forming a large pinwheel with prosciutto inside; secure with wooden toothpicks. Repeat with other strips forming 4 pinwheels.

For Sauce: In a small mixing bowl stir together all sauce ingredients.

To Cook by Indirect Grill Method: Brush pinwheels with sauce. In a covered grill arrange preheated coals around a drip pan. Test for *medium* heat above the pan.

Place pinwheels on the grill rack over the drip pan. Cover and grill for 11 to 13 minutes or till chicken is tender and no longer pink, turning once and brushing with sauce halfway through grilling time.

To Cook by Direct Grill Method: Brush pinwheels with sauce. Place pinwheels on the grill rack of an uncovered grill. Grill directly over *medium* coals about 10 minutes or till chicken is tender and no longer pink, turning once and brushing with sauce halfway through grilling time.

Per serving: 218 calories / 25 g protein / 0 g carbohydrate / 12 g fat (2 g saturated) / 59 mg cholesterol / 371 mg sodium / 181 mg potassium.

Basil-and-Garlic-Stuffed Chicken Breasts

Indirect or Direct Grilling   Serves 4

Stuffing:	¼ cup grated Parmesan cheese
	2 to 3 tablespoons snipped fresh basil *or* 2 teaspoons dried basil, crushed
	1 tablespoon margarine *or* butter, melted
	2 cloves garlic, minced
Poultry:	4 skinless, boneless chicken breast halves (about 1 pound total)
Sauce:	½ teaspoon finely shredded lemon peel
	2 tablespoons lemon juice
	1 tablespoon margarine *or* butter, melted

Simplify dinnertime chores—pound, roll, and stuff the chicken breasts ahead of time. Then, chill the rolled breasts till you are ready to grill them.

For Stuffing: In a small mixing bowl combine all stuffing ingredients. Set aside.

To Prepare Poultry: Rinse chicken; pat dry. Place *each* breast half between 2 pieces of plastic wrap. Working from the center to the edges, pound lightly with the flat side of a meat mallet to ⅛-inch thickness. Remove plastic wrap. Spread stuffing on chicken. Fold in sides of each chicken breast; roll up jelly-roll style, pressing edges to seal. Fasten with wooden toothpicks.

For Sauce: In a small mixing bowl combine all sauce ingredients.

To Cook by Indirect Grill Method: In a covered grill arrange preheated coals around a drip pan. Test for *medium* heat above the pan. Place chicken on the grill rack over the drip pan. Cover and grill for 20 to 25 minutes or till chicken is tender and no longer pink, brushing occasionally with sauce the last 10 minutes of grilling.

To Cook by Direct Grill Method: Place chicken on the grill rack of an uncovered grill. Grill directly over *medium* coals for 18 to 20 minutes or till chicken is tender and no longer pink, turning once halfway through grilling time and brushing occasionally with sauce the last 10 minutes of grilling.

Per serving: 205 calories / 24 g protein / 2 g carbohydrate / 11 g fat (3 g saturated) / 64 mg cholesterol / 238 mg sodium / 204 mg potassium.

Ginger-Marinated Turkey Steaks

| Indirect or Direct Grilling | Marinating Time: 6 to 24 hours | Serves 4 |

Marinade:	2 green onions, sliced (¼ cup)
	2 tablespoons soy sauce
	2 tablespoons cooking oil
	2 tablespoons dry sherry
	2 teaspoons lemon juice
	½ teaspoon grated gingerroot
	1 clove garlic, minced
	Dash pepper
Poultry:	4 turkey breast tenderloin steaks (about 1 pound total)

Accent each serving with a green onion brush and a radish fan.

For Marinade: In a small mixing bowl combine all marinade ingredients.

To Prepare Poultry: Rinse turkey; pat dry. Place turkey in a plastic bag set into a deep bowl. Pour marinade over turkey in bag. Seal bag and turn turkey to coat well. Marinate in the refrigerator for 6 to 24 hours, turning bag occasionally. Remove turkey from bag, reserving marinade.

To Cook by Indirect Grill Method: In a covered grill arrange preheated coals around a drip pan. Test for *medium* heat above the pan. Place turkey on the grill rack over the drip pan. Cover and grill for 15 to 18 minutes or till turkey is tender and no longer pink, brushing with reserved marinade halfway through the grilling time.

To Cook by Direct Grill Method: Brush turkey steaks with marinade. Place turkey on the grill rack of an uncovered grill. Grill directly over *medium* coals for 12 to 15 minutes or till turkey is tender and no longer pink, turning once and brushing with reserved marinade halfway through the grilling time.

Per serving: 151 calories / 22 g protein / 1 g carbohydrate / 6 g fat (1 g saturated) / 50 mg cholesterol / 303 mg sodium / 236 mg potassium.

Turkey with Ginger Salsa

Indirect and Direct Grilling	Marinating Time: 6 to 24 hours	Serves 4

Marinade:	¼ cup vinegar
	2 tablespoons dry sherry
	2 tablespoons soy sauce
	1 tablespoon grated gingerroot
	1 clove garlic, minced
	1 teaspoon crushed red pepper
Poultry:	4 turkey breast tenderloin steaks (about 1 pound total)
Salsa:	1 medium tomato, peeled, seeded, and chopped
	1 green onion, sliced (2 tablespoons)
	¼ cup chopped green pepper
	1 tablespoon snipped cilantro
Accompaniment:	4 6-inch flour tortillas

Stirring a little of the ginger marinade into fresh tomato salsa creates a flavorful poultry relish.

For Marinade: In a small mixing bowl combine all marinade ingredients. Reserve *2 tablespoons* of the marinade for salsa.

To Prepare Poultry: Rinse turkey; pat dry. Place turkey in a plastic bag set into a deep bowl. Pour marinade over turkey in bag. Seal bag and turn turkey to coat well. Marinate in the refrigerator for 6 to 24 hours, turning bag occasionally. Remove turkey from bag, reserving marinade.

For Salsa: In a small mixing bowl combine all the salsa ingredients and the 2 tablespoons reserved marinade. (*Do not use the mixture in which turkey was marinated.*) Cover and chill salsa till serving time.

To Cook by Indirect Grill Method: In a covered grill arrange preheated coals around a drip pan. Test for *medium* heat above the pan. Place turkey on the grill rack over the drip pan. Cover and grill for 15 to 18 minutes or till turkey is tender and no longer pink, brushing with marinade after 10 minutes.

To Cook by Direct Grill Method: Place turkey on the grill rack of an uncovered grill. Grill directly over *medium* coals for 12 to 15 minutes or till turkey is tender and no longer pink, turning once and brushing with reserved marinade halfway through grilling time.

To Serve: Place tortillas in a single layer on the grill rack for 1 minute. Serve turkey with warmed tortillas and chilled salsa.

Per serving: 208 calories / 24 g protein / 18 g carbohydrate / 4 g fat (1 g saturated) / 50 mg cholesterol / 564 mg sodium / 347 mg potassium.

Double-Glazed Turkey Breasts

Double-Glazed Turkey Breasts

Indirect Grilling   Serves 10

Wood Chips:	4	cups hickory wood chips *or* mesquite wood chips (optional)
Five-Spice Glaze:	⅓	cup orange marmalade
	1	tablespoon hoisin sauce
	¼	teaspoon five-spice powder
	¼	teaspoon garlic powder
Honey-Mustard Glaze:	¼	cup honey
	1	tablespoon Dijon-style mustard
	1	tablespoon white wine Worcestershire sauce
	1	tablespoon margarine *or* butter, melted
Poultry:	2	2- to 2½-pound turkey breast halves
	1	tablespoon cooking oil

Two recipes in one! Each turkey breast half is brushed with a different glaze.

To Prepare Wood Chips: If using, at least 1 hour before grilling, soak wood chips in enough water to cover. Drain chips before using.

For Five-Spice Glaze: In a small mixing bowl stir together all of the ingredients. Set aside.

For Honey-Mustard Glaze: In a small mixing bowl stir together all the ingredients. Set aside.

To Prepare Turkey: Remove bone from turkey breasts. Rinse turkey; pat dry. Brush turkey with oil. Insert a meat thermometer into the center of one of the turkey breasts.

To Cook by Indirect Grill Method: In a covered grill arrange preheated coals for indirect cooking. Test for *medium* heat where turkey will cook. If using, sprinkle *1 cup* of the drained wood chips onto the preheated coals. Place the turkey breasts, side by side, on a rack in a roasting pan on the grill rack. Cover and grill for 1½ to 2 hours or till thermometer registers 170°, brushing one breast half with Five-Spice Glaze and the other breast half with Honey-Mustard Glaze several times during the last 15 minutes of grilling. Add additional coals and drained wood chips, if using, every 20 to 30 minutes or as necessary to maintain medium heat.

To Serve: Heat any of the remaining glazes. Pass the glazes with the sliced turkey.

Per serving: 171 calories / 16 g protein / 15 g carbohydrate / 5 g fat (1 g saturated) / 40 mg cholesterol / 150 mg sodium / 179 mg potassium.

Mustard-Glazed Turkey Drumsticks

Indirect Grilling   Serves 4

For Glaze:	¼ cup coarse-grain brown mustard, hot-style mustard, horseradish mustard, *or* sweet-hot mustard
	1 tablespoon vinegar
Poultry:	2 turkey drumsticks (1 to 1½ pounds each)
	1 to 2 tablespoons cooking oil

Stir together mustard and vinegar for an almost-instant glaze.

For Glaze: In a small mixing bowl stir together glaze ingredients. Set aside.

Prepare turkey: Remove skin from turkey drumsticks. Rinse drumsticks; pat dry. Brush drumsticks with oil.

To Cook by Indirect Grill Method: In a covered grill arrange preheated coals for indirect cooking. Test for *medium* heat where turkey will cook. Place turkey on a rack in a roasting pan on the grill rack. Cover and grill 1 to 1¼ hours or till turkey is tender and no longer pink, turning once and brushing occasionally with glaze after 30 minutes.

To Serve: Cut the meat from the drumsticks.

Per serving: 213 calories / 22 g protein / 1 g carbohydrate / 13 g fat (3 g saturated) / 68 mg cholesterol / 262 mg sodium / 233 mg potassium.

Cranberry-Glazed Turkey Drumsticks

Indirect Grilling   Serves 4

Sauce:	1	16-ounce can whole cranberry sauce
	½	cup apricot preserves
	2	tablespoons lemon juice
Poultry:	2	turkey drumsticks (1 to 1½ pounds each) *or* 8 chicken drumsticks
		(about 1½ pounds total)
	1	tablespoon cooking oil

We suggest half of a turkey drumstick per serving, but you may want to serve whole ones to those who crave dark meat and possess hearty appetites.

For Sauce: In a small saucepan combine all sauce ingredients. Cook and stir till bubbly. Remove from heat; set aside.

To Prepare Poultry: Remove skin from turkey or chicken drumsticks. Rinse turkey or chicken; pat dry. Brush with oil.

To Cook by Indirect Grill Method: In a covered grill arrange preheated coals for indirect cooking. Test for *medium* heat where turkey will cook. Place turkey on a rack in a pan on the grill rack. (Place chicken on the grill rack above a drip pan.) Cover and grill for 1¾ to 2 hours for turkey or 50 to 60 minutes for chicken or till poultry is tender and no longer pink, brushing frequently with sauce the last 10 minutes of grilling.

To Serve: Heat remaining sauce. Cut the meat from the turkey drumsticks. Serve turkey or chicken with sauce.

Per serving: 543 calories / 35 g protein / 73 g carbohydrate / 12 g fat (4 g saturated) / 107 mg cholesterol / 133 mg sodium / 426 mg potassium.

Cider-Glazed Turkey Thighs
with Sweet Potatoes

Cider-Glazed Turkey Thighs with Sweet Potatoes

Indirect Grilling   Serves 4

Sauce:	½ cup apple cider *or* apple juice
	2 tablespoons apple jelly
	1 teaspoon cornstarch
	¼ teaspoon ground nutmeg
Sweet Potatoes:	12 ounces sweet potatoes (about 2 medium), peeled and cut into ½-inch-thick slices
	2 medium apples, cut in wedges
Poultry:	2 small turkey thighs (2 pounds total)

Candied sweet potatoes and apples cook along side the turkey thighs in this traditional combination.

For Sauce: In a small saucepan stir together all sauce ingredients. Cook and stir till thickened and bubbly. Cook and stir for 2 minutes more. Remove from heat; set aside.

To Prepare Sweet Potatoes: Toss together sweet potatoes and apples. Tear off a 36x18-inch piece of heavy foil. Fold in half to make a double thickness of foil that measures 18x18 inches. Place sweet potato mixture in the center of the foil. Drizzle with *half* of the sauce. Bring up two opposite edges of foil and seal with a double fold. Then fold remaining ends to completely encase the packet, leaving space for steam to build. Refrigerate the packet till ready to grill.

To Prepare Poultry: Remove skin from turkey thighs, if desired. Rinse turkey; pat dry. Insert meat thermometer into the center of one of the turkey thighs, not touching bone.

To Cook by Indirect Grill Method: In a covered grill arrange preheated coals for indirect cooking. Test for *medium* heat where turkey will cook. Place turkey thighs, bone side down, on rack in a roasting pan on the grill rack. Cover and grill for 1¼ to 1¾ hours or till a thermometer inserted in the thickest portion of the thighs registers 180° to 185°, brushing frequently with sauce the last 10 minutes of grilling. Place the foil packet containing the sweet potatoes beside the pan with turkey thighs on the grill rack, not over coals. Grill foil packet the last 30 to 40 minutes of grilling.

To Serve: Cut the turkey meat from the bones. Serve with sweet potatoes.

Per serving: 354 calories / 35 g protein / 37 g carbohydrate / 7 g fat (2 g saturated) / 83 mg cholesterol / 105 mg sodium / 655 mg potassium.

Chicken Patties with Fresh Tomato Sauce

Indirect or Direct Grilling   Serves 4

Poultry Mixture:	1	beaten egg
	½	cup soft bread crumbs
	¼	cup chopped walnuts, toasted
	2	tablespoons grated Parmesan cheese
	1	green onion, thinly sliced (2 tablespoons)
	2	teaspoons snipped fresh basil *or* ½ teaspoon dried basil, crushed
	¼	teaspoon salt
	⅛	teaspoon pepper
	1	pound ground raw chicken *or* ground raw turkey
	¼	teaspoon salt
Toppings:	¼	cup plain low-fat yogurt
	1	small tomato, chopped (⅔ cup)

Another time, slip the patties into pita bread rounds. Then, spoon on the yogurt and sprinkle with chopped tomatoes.

To Prepare Poultry Mixture: In a medium mixing bowl combine all poultry mixture ingredients *except* chicken or turkey. Add ground chicken or turkey and mix well. Shape the mixture into four ¾-inch-thick patties.

To Cook by Indirect Grill Method: In a covered grill arrange preheated coals around a drip pan. Test for *medium* heat above the pan. Place patties on the grill rack over the drip pan. Cover and grill for 20 to 24 minutes or till juices run clear, turning once halfway through grilling time.

To Cook by Direct Grill Method: Grill patties on the grill rack of an uncovered grill directly over *medium* coals for 14 to 18 minutes or till juices run clear, turning once halfway through grilling time.

To Serve: Spoon yogurt over patties and top with chopped tomatoes.

Per serving: 232 calories / 21 g protein / 7 g carbohydrate / 13 g fat (3 g saturated) / 111 mg cholesterol / 304 mg sodium / 310 mg potassium.

Teriyaki Turkey Patties

Indirect or Direct Grilling   Serves 4

Poultry Mixture:	1	beaten egg
	½	cup soft bread crumbs
	¼	cup chopped water chestnuts
	2	tablespoons chopped onion
	1	tablespoon teriyaki sauce
	1	pound ground raw turkey
Sauce:	¼	cup orange marmalade
	1	tablespoon teriyaki sauce
	½	teaspoon sesame seed

Chopped water chestnuts add just the right amount of crunch to these extraordinary orange-glazed turkey burgers.

To Prepare Poultry Mixture: In a medium mixing bowl combine all poultry mixture ingredients *except* turkey. Add ground turkey and mix well. Shape the mixture into four ¾-inch-thick patties. (Mixture will be soft.)

To Cook by Indirect Grill Method: In a covered grill arrange preheated coals around a drip pan. Test for *medium* heat above the pan. Place patties on the grill rack over the drip pan. Cover and grill for 20 to 24 minutes or till juices run clear, turning once halfway through grilling time.

To Cook by Direct Grill Method: Grill patties on the grill rack of an uncovered grill directly over *medium* coals for 14 to 18 minutes or till juices run clear, turning once halfway through grilling time.

For Sauce: In a small saucepan combine all sauce ingredients. Cook over low heat till marmalade melts, stirring occasionally. Spoon sauce over cooked patties.

Picnic Pointers

Although barbecuing in the backyard is fun, picnicing in the park can be a real summer treat. To ensure that your food is as fresh and tasty at the picnic site as it was before you set out, keep these hints in mind.

Keep all work surfaces, utensils, and your hands immaculate during food preparation so harmful bacteria won't be transferred to the picnic foods. Use bottled mayonnaise or salad dressing rather than homemade for salads and sandwiches. The acidity of commercial mayonnaise helps prevent food spoilage.

Make sure all meat is thoroughly cooked and chilled. Always refrigerate meat as soon as it is cooked. Don't wait for it to cool to room temperature before refrigerating.

Put tightly wrapped and well-chilled raw meats for grilling in the bottom of the cooler. Pack your cooler so the food to be eaten first is on top. This way you avoid unpacking and repacking the food outdoors. Use ice packs or blocks of ice because they last longer than ice cubes. Avoid dry ice because it causes freezer burn of food and bare skin.

Look for a shade tree to set your cooler under. It's very easy for cold foods to warm up quickly when sitting in the hot sunlight, even if they are stored in an insulated chest.

Urge everyone to bring along a hearty appetite to eliminate leftovers. Don't carry home leftovers—discard them. Any food that has been exposed to sunshine or warm temperatures can be harmful, even though it may still look appetizing.

Per serving: 240 calories / 18 g protein / 19 g carbohydrate / 10 g fat (3 g saturated) / 95 mg cholesterol / 400 mg sodium / 230 mg potassium.

Thai Turkey Bundles

Indirect or Direct Grilling   Serves 6

Dipping Sauce:	¼	cup lemon juice
	3	tablespoons fish sauce
	1	tablespoon snipped cilantro
	2	teaspoons sugar
	1	teaspoon soy sauce
	¼ to ½	teaspoon crushed red pepper
	½	teaspoon toasted sesame oil
Poultry Mixture:	1	beaten egg
	½	cup coarsely chopped water chestnuts
	⅓	cup fine dry bread crumbs
	1	green onion, finely chopped (2 tablespoons)
	1	tablespoon soy sauce
	1	tablespoon lemon juice
	2	teaspoons grated gingerroot
	½	teaspoon sugar
	¼	teaspoon salt
	¼	teaspoon chili oil *or* a dash ground red pepper
	1½	pounds ground raw turkey
	12	small savoy cabbage leaves *or* small leaf lettuce leaves

Ruffly savoy cabbage leaves encase these spiced turkey loaves. Use leaf lettuce if you can't find the cabbage.

For Dipping Sauce: In a small mixing bowl stir together all the dipping sauce ingredients. Set aside.

To Prepare Poultry Mixture: In a large mixing bowl combine all poultry mixture ingredients *except* turkey and cabbage or lettuce leaves. Add ground turkey and mix well. Shape the mixture into twelve 4x1½x¾-inch loaves.

To Cook by Indirect Grill Method: In a covered grill arrange preheated coals around a drip pan. Test for *medium* heat above the pan. Place loaves on the grill rack over the drip pan. Cover and grill for 18 to 20 minutes or till juices run clear, turning once halfway through grilling time.

To Cook by Direct Grill Method: Grill loaves on the grill rack of an uncovered grill directly over *medium* coals for 14 to 18 minutes or till juices run clear, turning once halfway through grilling time.

To Serve: Wrap each loaf in a savoy cabbage leaf or lettuce leaf. Serve with dipping sauce.

Per serving: 210 calories / 18 g protein / 11 g carbohydrate / 10 g fat (3 g saturated) / 78 mg cholesterol / 876 mg sodium / 269 mg potassium.

Thai Turkey Bundles

Turkey with Wild Rice Dressing

Indirect Grilling   Serves 8

Wood Chips:	4 cups hickory chips (optional)
Dressing:	½ cup wild rice
	2¼ cups water
	½ cup brown rice
	1 tablespoon instant chicken bouillon granules
	½ teaspoon ground sage
	2 cups sliced fresh mushrooms
	1 medium onion, chopped (½ cup)
	4 slices bacon, crisp-cooked, drained, and crumbled
	½ cup slivered almonds, toasted
Poultry:	1 8- to 10-pound turkey
	Cooking oil
Glaze:	¼ cup currant jelly

Fire up the grill and begin a new Thanksgiving tradition with this succulent bird and an elegant wild rice dressing.

To Prepare Wood Chips: If using, 1 hour before grilling, soak wood chips in enough water to cover. Drain chips before using.

For Dressing: Rinse wild rice in a strainer under *cold* water about 1 minute. In a medium saucepan combine wild rice, water, brown rice, bouillon granules, and sage. Bring to boiling; reduce heat. Cover and simmer for 45 minutes. Add mushrooms and onion. Cook, covered, for 10 to 20 minutes more or till vegetables and rice are tender, stirring frequently. Stir in bacon and almonds.

Tear off a 48x18-inch piece of heavy foil. Fold in half to make a double thickness of foil that measures 24x18 inches. Place dressing in the center of the foil. Bring up two opposite edges of foil and seal with a double fold. Then fold remaining ends to completely enclose the dressing, leaving space for steam to build. Refrigerate the packet..

To Prepare Turkey: Remove neck and giblets from turkey. Rinse the turkey; pat dry. Skewer the neck skin to the back. Tuck drumsticks under the band of skin across the tail. Twist wing tips under the back. Insert a meat thermometer into the center of the inside thigh muscle, not touching the bone.

To Cook by Indirect Grill Method: In a covered grill arrange preheated coals for indirect cooking. Test for *medium* heat where turkey will cook. If using, sprinkle *1 cup* drained wood chips onto preheated coals. Place turkey, breast side up, on a rack in a roasting pan on the grill rack. Brush turkey with cooking oil. Cover and grill for 2½ to 3½ hours or till meat thermometer registers 180° to 185°. Add additional coals and drained wood chips, if using, every 20 to 30 minutes or as necessary.

Place foil packet of dressing beside turkey on grill rack. Grill directly over *medium* to *medium-high* coals the last 30 to 35 minutes of grilling. Fluff with fork before serving.

For Glaze: In a saucepan melt jelly.

To Serve: Remove turkey from grill. Brush with melted jelly. Let stand, covered, for 15 minutes before carving. Serve with dressing.

Per serving: 342 calories / 39 g protein / 21 g carbohydrate / 11 g fat (3 g saturated) / 93 mg cholesterol / 389 mg sodium / 539 mg potassium.

Savory Grilled Turkey with Summer Squash

Indirect Grilling   Serves 8

Wood Chips:	4 cups hickory *or* other wood chips (optional)
Accompaniment:	Summer Squash Casserole (see recipe, page 170)
Poultry:	1 6- to 8-pound fresh turkey *or* frozen turkey, thawed
	4 cloves elephant garlic, halved *or* 8 to 10 regular garlic cloves (optional)
	Cooking oil

Stuffing the bird with garlic produces a subtle trace of flavor in every bite.

To Prepare Wood Chips: If using, at least 1 hour before grilling, soak wood chips in enough water to cover. Drain the chips before using.

To Prepare Accompaniment: Prepare Summer Squash Casserole. Refrigerate the packets till ready to grill.

To Prepare Turkey: Remove the neck and giblets from turkey. Rinse the turkey on the outside as well as inside the body and neck cavities. Pat turkey dry with paper towels. Skewer the neck skin to the back. If desired, place garlic in the body cavity. Tuck drumsticks under the band of skin across the tail. Twist wing tips under the back. Insert a meat thermometer into the center of the inside thigh muscle, not touching the bone.

To Cook by Indirect Grill Method: In a covered grill arrange preheated coals for indirect cooking. Test for *medium* heat where turkey will cook. If using, sprinkle *1 cup* of

the drained wood chips onto the preheated coals. Place the turkey, breast side up, on a rack in a roasting pan on the grill rack. Brush the turkey with cooking oil. Cover and grill for 1¾ to 2¼ hours or till meat thermometer registers 180° to 185°, brushing occasionally with cooking oil. Add additional coals and drained wood chips, if using, every 20 to 30 minutes or as necessary. Place the foil packet of Summer Squash Casserole beside the turkey on the grill rack. Grill foil packet directly over *medium-high* coals the last 20 minutes of grilling.

To Serve: Remove turkey from the grill. Let turkey stand, covered, for 15 minutes before carving. Serve with Summer Squash Casserole.

Per serving: 275 calories / 42 g protein / 1 g carbohydrate / 10 g fat (3 g saturated) / 108 mg cholesterol / 101 mg sodium / 435 mg potassium.

Honey-Soy Grilled Chicken

Indirect Grilling	Marinating Time: 6 to 24 hours	Serves 4

Marinade:		
	¼	cup water
	¼	cup soy sauce
	¼	cup dry sherry
	1	green onion, sliced (2 tablespoons)
	2	cloves garlic, minced
	½	teaspoon five-spice powder
Poultry:	1	2½- to 3-pound whole broiler-fryer chicken
	1	tablespoon cooking oil
	1	tablespoon honey

Brushing the chicken with oil before grilling results in skin that's crisp and tender.

To Prepare Marinade: In a small mixing bowl combine all marinade ingredients.

To Prepare Poultry: Remove the neck and giblets from chicken. Rinse the chicken on the outside as well as inside the body and neck cavities. Pat chicken dry with paper towels. Skewer the neck skin to the back. Twist wing tips under the back. Place chicken in a plastic bag set into a deep bowl. Pour marinade over chicken in bag. Seal bag and turn chicken to coat well. Marinate in the refrigerator for 6 to 24 hours, turning bag occasionally. Remove chicken from bag and discard marinade. Brush chicken with oil.

To Cook by Indirect Grill Method: In a covered grill arrange preheated coals for indirect cooking. Test for *medium* heat where chicken will cook. Place the chicken, breast side up, on a rack in a roasting pan on the grill rack. Cover and grill for 1 to 1¼ hours or till chicken is no longer pink and the drumsticks move easily in their sockets, brushing with honey during the last 10 minutes of grilling.

Per serving: 285 calories / 31 g protein / 5 g carbohydrate / 15 g fat (4 g saturated) / 98 mg cholesterol / 349 mg sodium / 259 mg potassium.

Honey-Soy Grilled Chicken

Herbed Cornish Game Hens with Vegetables

Indirect Grilling   Serves 4

Poultry:	2	1¼- to 1½-pound Cornish game hens (thawed, if frozen)
Vegetables:	4	medium parsnips, cut into 2-inch pieces
	4	medium carrots, cut into 2-inch pieces
	4	leeks, cut into 2-inch pieces
Sauce:	6	tablespoons margarine *or* butter
	1	teaspoon dried sage, crushed
	½	teaspoon dried thyme, crushed
	¼	teaspoon salt
	¼	teaspoon pepper
	2	teaspoons lemon juice

Sage and thyme flavor both the hens and a packet full of parsnips, leeks, and carrots.

To Prepare Poultry: Rinse hens; pat dry. Pull neck skin, if present, to back of each hen. Twist wing tips under back, holding skin in place. Tie legs to tail.

To Prepare Vegetables: Cook parsnips, carrots, and leeks in a small amount of boiling water for 10 minutes. Drain and set aside.

For Sauce: In a small saucepan combine all sauce ingredients. Cook over low heat till the margarine is melted.

To Cook by Indirect Grill Method: In a covered grill arrange preheated coals for indirect cooking. Test for *medium* heat where hens will cook. Place hens, breast side up, on a rack in a roasting pan on the grill rack. Brush hens with some of the sauce. Cover and grill for 1 to 1¼ hours or till tender and no longer pink, brushing occasionally with sauce. Place vegetables on a large piece of heavy foil; fold edges up to form a pan. Brush with sauce. Add vegetables the last 5 minutes of grilling, placing them on the grill rack directly over the coals. Brush vegetables occasionally with sauce.

To Serve: Cut hens in half lengthwise. Serve with vegetables.

Per serving: 541 calories / 33 g protein / 29 g carbohydrate / 34 g fat (7 g saturated) / 100 mg cholesterol / 443 mg sodium / 530 mg potassium.

Zippy Cornish Game Hens

Indirect Grilling	Marinating Time: 6 to 24 hours	Serves 4

Marinade:	½	cup water
	½	of a 5-ounce jar prepared horseradish (¼ cup)
	2	tablespoons lemon juice
	1	teaspoon coarsely ground pepper
	½	teaspoon ground allspice
Poultry:	2	1¼- to 1½-pound Cornish game hens, halved lenthwise (thawed, if frozen)
Sauce:	¼	cup margarine or butter, melted
	1	teaspoon finely shredded lemon peel
		Prepared horseradish (optional)

Horseradish, pepper, and allspice give these marinated game hens their "zip."

For Marinade: In a small mixing bowl combine all marinade ingredients. Set aside.

To Prepare Cornish Hens: If desired, remove skin from hens. Rinse hens; pat dry. Place hens in a plastic bag set into a deep bowl. Pour marinade over hens in bag. Seal bag and turn hens to coat well. Marinate in the refrigerator for 6 to 24 hours, turning bag occasionally. Remove hens from bag; discard the marinade.

For Sauce: In a small saucepan melt margarine or butter. Stir in lemon peel.

To Cook by Indirect Grill Method: In a covered grill arrange preheated coals for indirect cooking. Test for *medium* heat where hens will cook. Place hens, bone side down, on a rack in a roasting pan on the grill rack. Cover and grill about 1 hour or till meat is tender and no longer pink, brushing occasionally with sauce. If desired, serve with additional horseradish.

Per serving: 250 calories / 15 g protein / 1 g carbohydrate / 21 g fat (4 g saturated) / 50 mg cholesterol / 259 mg sodium / 35 mg potassium.

Cornish Hens with Fruited Stuffing

Indirect Grilling   Serves 4

Stuffing:	3	cups whole wheat bread cubes (about 4 slices)
	2	medium apples, peeled, cored, and chopped (1½ cups)
	¼	cups dried cranberries *or* cherries *or* raisins
	¼	teaspoon ground cinnamon
		Dash ground cloves
	½	cup apple juice
Glaze:	½	cup apple jelly
	1	tablespoon apple juice
	½	teaspoon ground cinnamon
Poultry:	2	1¼- to 1½-pound Cornish game hens (thawed, if frozen)

Serve these apple-cinnamon glazed birds for a hearty autumn meal.

For Stuffing: In a medium mixing bowl combine all stuffing ingredients *except* apple juice. Stir in apple juice.

Tear off a 36x18-inch piece of heavy foil. Fold in half to make a double thickness of foil that measures 18x18 inches. Place stuffing in the center of the foil. Bring up two opposite edges of foil and seal with a double fold. Then fold remaining ends to completely enclose the stuffing, leaving space for steam to build. Refrigerate the packet till ready to grill.

For Glaze: In a small saucepan combine all sauce ingredients. Heat till jelly is melted, stirring occasionally. Set aside.

To Prepare Poultry: Rinse hens; pat dry. Pull neck skin, if present, to back of each hen. Twist wing tips under back, holding skin in place. Tie legs to tail.

To Cook by Indirect Grill Method: In a covered grill arrange preheated coals for indirect cooking. Test for *medium* heat where hens will cook. Place hens, breast side up, on a rack in a roasting pan on the grill rack. Cover and grill for 1 to 1¼ hours or till tender and no longer pink, brushing occasionally with glaze the last 15 minutes of grilling. Place the foil packet of stuffing beside the hens on the grill rack. Grill foil packet directly over *medium* to *medium-high* coals the last 15 to 20 minutes of grilling.

To Serve: Cut hens in half lengthwise. Serve with stuffing.

Per serving: 537 calories / 33 g protein / 60 g carbohydrate / 20 g fat (4 g saturated) / 100 mg cholesterol / 262 mg sodium / 205 mg potassium.

Cornish Hens with Fruited Stuffing

Savory Wine-Marinated Pheasant

Indirect Grilling | Marinating Time: 6 to 24 hours | Serves 4

Marinade:	1 small onion, thinly sliced
	¾ cup dry white wine
	¼ cup lime juice *or* lemon juice
	3 tablespoons snipped parsley
	2 tablespoons cooking oil
	¼ teaspoon salt
	¼ teaspoon bottled hot pepper sauce
	½ teaspoon dried savory, crushed
Poultry:	1 2- to 2½-pound domestic pheasant, quartered

Look for domestic pheasant with the frozen turkeys in large supermarkets or specialty stores.

For Marinade: In a small mixing bowl combine all marinade ingredients.

To Prepare Poultry: Rinse pheasant; pat dry. Place pheasant in a plastic bag set into a deep bowl. Pour marinade over pheasant in bag. Seal bag and turn pheasant to coat well. Marinate in the refrigerator for 6 to 24 hours, turning bag occasionally. Remove pheasant from bag, reserving marinade.

To Cook by Indirect Grill Method: In a covered grill arrange preheated coals around a drip pan. Test for *medium* heat above the pan. Place pheasant, bone side down, on the grill rack over the drip pan. Cover and grill for

25 to 30 minutes or till pheasant is tender and no longer pink, brushing occasionally with reserved marinade during the first 15 minutes.

To Serve: While pheasant cooks, place marinade in medium saucepan. Bring to boiling; reduce heat. Cover and simmer for 12 to 15 minutes or till onions are tender. Use a slotted spoon to serve onions over pheasant.

Per serving: 239 calories / 20 g protein / 3 g carbohydrate / 13 g fat (3 g saturated) / 53 mg cholesterol / 182 mg sodium / 290 mg potassium.

MOUTH-WATERING MEATS

If you'd like to expand your barbecue reportoire beyond

burgers and 'dogs, read on for some juicy alternatives!

Bite into Tequila-Lime Fajitas, Grilled Rump Roast,

and Cajun-Style Pork Chops.

Grilled Basil Burgers

Indirect or Direct Grilling   Serves 8

Meat Mixture:	1	beaten egg
	⅔	cup chopped onion
	½	cup grated Parmesan cheese
	¼	cup snipped fresh basil *or* 1 tablespoon dried basil, crushed
	¼	cup catsup
	2	cloves garlic, minced
	¼	teaspoon salt
	¼	teaspoon pepper
	1	pound lean ground beef
	1	pound ground raw turkey
Bread:	8	hamburger buns
Toppings:	8	tomato slices

Cook the number of burgers you need, then individually wrap the uncooked patties in freezer wrap and freeze for up to 3 months. Next time you want to serve burgers, thaw the frozen patties overnight in the refrigerator and presto—they're ready for grilling.

To Prepare Meat Mixture: In a medium mixing bowl combine all meat mixture ingredients *except* beef and turkey. Add ground beef and turkey and mix well. Shape mixture into eight ¾-inch-thick-patties.

To Cook by Indirect Grill Method: In a covered grill arrange preheated coals around drip pan. Test for *medium* heat above the pan. Place meat on the grill over the drip pan. Cover and grill for 20 to 24 minutes or till no pink remains, turning once halfway through grilling time.

To Cook by Direct Grill Method: Grill meat on the grill rack of an uncovered grill directly over *medium* coals for 14 to 18 minutes or till no pink remains, turning once halfway through grilling time.

To Serve: Split buns and toast on the grill. Serve patties in buns with tomato slices.

Per serving: 333 calories / 25 g protein / 25 g carbohydrate / 14 g fat (5 g saturated) / 88 mg cholesterol / 570 mg sodium / 349 mg potassium.

Double-Beef Burgers

Indirect or Direct Grilling   Serves 4

Meat Mixture:	1	beaten egg
	1	2½-ounce package very thinly sliced fully cooked corned beef, chopped
	⅓	cup finely chopped cabbage
	¼	cup soft rye bread crumbs (about ½ slice)
	½	teaspoon caraway seed
	¼	teaspoon salt
	1	pound lean ground beef
Bread:	8	slices rye bread
Toppings:	3	tablespoons horseradish mustard
	4	small kale, cabbage, *or* lettuce leaves

Hidden within these beefy burgers are all the makings of a Reuben sandwich—corned beef, cabbage, and rye bread.

To Prepare Meat Mixture: In a medium mixing bowl combine all meat mixture ingredients *except* ground beef. Add ground beef and mix well. Shape mixture into four ¾-inch-thick patties.

To Cook by Indirect Grill Method: In a covered grill arrange preheated coals around a drip pan. Test for *medium* heat above the pan. Place meat on the grill rack over the drip pan. Cover and grill for 20 to 24 minutes or till no pink remains, turning once halfway through grilling time.

To Cook by Direct Grill Method: Grill meat on the grill rack of an uncovered grill directly over *medium* coals for 14 to 18 minutes or till no pink remains, turning once halfway through grilling time.

To Serve: Toast the bread on the grill. Spread toasted bread slices with horseradish mustard. Serve patties on bread slice; top each burger with a kale leaf and second bread slice.

Per serving: 376 calories / 31 g protein / 29 g carbohydrate / 16 g fat (5 g saturated) / 135 mg cholesterol / 883 mg sodium / 416 mg potassium.

Feta-Stuffed Pita Burgers

Feta-Stuffed Pita Burgers

Indirect or Direct Grilling   Serves 4

Meat Mixture:	2 tablespoons cornmeal
	2 tablespoons milk
	1 tablespoon finely chopped onion
	1 clove garlic, minced
	¼ teaspoon salt
	¼ teaspoon dried oregano, crushed
	⅛ teaspoon lemon-pepper seasoning
	8 ounces lean ground lamb
	8 ounces lean ground beef
Filling:	⅓ cup finely crumbled feta cheese
	1 tablespoon milk
Seasoning:	¼ teaspoon ground cumin
	¼ teaspoon ground red pepper
Bread:	2 large pita bread rounds
Toppings:	2 cups shredded fresh spinach

Greek it is! This seasoned lamb and beef burger is filled with feta, then tucked in a pita along with fresh spinach.

To Prepare Meat Mixture: In a medium mixing bowl combine all meat mixture ingredients *except* lamb and beef. Add ground lamb and beef and mix well. Shape mixture into eight ¼-inch-thick patties (about 4-inch diameter).

For Filling: In a small mixing bowl combine feta and milk. Place *1 tablespoon* feta mixture in centers of 4 of the patties. Top with remaining patties; press edges to seal.

For Seasoning: In a small bowl combine seasoning ingredients. Sprinkle seasoning mixture over patties.

To Cook by Indirect Grill Method: In a covered grill arrange preheated coals around a drip pan. Test for *medium* heat above the pan. Place meat on the grill rack over the drip pan. Cover and grill for 18 to 22 minutes or till no pink remains, turning once halfway through grilling time.

To Cook by Direct Grill Method: Grill meat on the grill rack of an uncovered grill directly over *medium* coals for 12 to 16 minutes or till no pink remains, turning once halfway through grilling time.

To Serve: Split pita bread rounds in half crosswise. Serve meat patties in pita halves with spinach.

Per serving: 314 calories / 25 g protein / 16 g carbohydrate / 16 g fat (7 g saturated) / 84 mg cholesterol / 475 mg sodium / 457 mg potassium.

Beef and Bulgur Burgers

Indirect or Direct Grilling   Serves 4

Meat Mixture:	1	slightly beaten egg white
	¼	cup bulgur
	¼	cup catsup
	1	tablespoon snipped parsley
	1	teaspoon dried Italian seasoning, crushed
	½	teaspoon garlic salt
	⅛	teaspoon pepper
	1	pound lean ground beef
Bread:	4	whole wheat hamburger buns
Toppings:		Lettuce leaves
	4	tomato slices
	¼	cup alfalfa sprouts

Want a good-for-you burger? Look no further. This hefty burger is loaded with fiber, but lower in fat and cholesterol than most other burgers.

To Prepare Meat Mixture: In a medium mixing bowl combine all meat mixture ingredients *except* beef. Add ground beef and mix well. Shape mixture into four ¾-inch-thick patties.

To Cook by Indirect Grill Method: In a covered grill arrange preheated coals around a drip pan. Test for *medium* heat above the pan. Place meat on the grill rack over the drip pan. Cover and grill for 20 to 24 minutes or till no pink remains, turning once halfway through grilling time.

To Cook by Direct Grill Method: Grill meat on the grill rack of an uncovered grill directly over *medium* coals for 14 to 18 minutes or till no pink remains, turning once halfway through grilling time.

To Serve: Split the buns and toast on the grill. Serve patties in buns with lettuce, tomato, and alfalfa sprouts.

Per serving: 355 calories / 26 g protein / 32 g carbohydrate / 13 g fat (5 g saturated) / 71 mg cholesterol / 694 mg sodium / 430 mg potassium.

Pickle Burgers

Indirect or Direct Grilling   Serves 4

Meat Mixture:	1	beaten egg
	⅓	cup finely chopped dill pickle
	¼	cup fine dry bread crumbs
	1	tablespoon horseradish mustard
	1	tablespoon catsup
	½	teaspoon onion salt
		Dash pepper
	1	pound lean ground beef
Bread:	4	hamburger buns
Toppings:	4	thin onion slices
	4	thin tomato slices

Chopped dill pickles are the surprise ingredients in this juicy burger.

To Prepare Meat Mixture: In a medium mixing bowl combine all meat mixture ingredients *except* beef. Add ground beef and mix well. Shape mixture into four ¾-inch-thick patties.

To Cook by Indirect Grill Method: In a covered grill arrange preheated coals around a drip pan. Test for *medium* heat above the pan. Place meat on the grill rack over the drip pan. Cover and grill for 20 to 24 minutes or till no pink remains, turning once halfway through grilling time.

To Cook by Direct Grill Method: Grill meat on the grill rack of an uncovered grill directly over *medium* coals for 14 to 18 minutes or till no pink remains, turning once halfway through grilling time.

To Serve: Split the buns and toast on the grill. Serve patties in buns with onion and tomato slices.

Per serving: 359 calories / 27 g protein / 29 g carbohydrate / 15 g fat (5 g saturated) / 125 mg cholesterol / 879 mg sodium / 386 mg potassium.

Pizza Burgers

Pizza Burgers

Indirect or Direct Grilling   Serves 4

Meat Mixture:	1	beaten egg
	⅓	cup chopped canned mushrooms, drained
	¼	cup seasoned fine dry bread crumbs
	2	tablespoons milk
	½	teaspoon dried Italian seasoning, crushed
	¼	teaspoon salt
	1	pound lean ground pork
Bread:	4	¾-inch-thick French bread slices
Toppings:	1	8-ounce can pizza sauce
	¼	cup sliced pitted ripe olives
	¼	cup shredded mozzarella cheese (1 ounce)

If it's a toss up between pizza and burgers, give this recipe a try.

To Prepare Meat Mixture: In a medium mixing bowl combine all meat mixture ingredients *except* pork. Add ground pork and mix well. Shape mixture into four ¾-inch-thick patties.

To Cook by Indirect Grill Method: In a covered grill arrange preheated coals around a drip pan. Test for *medium* heat above the pan. Place meat on the grill rack over the drip pan. Cover and grill for 20 to 24 minutes or till no pink remains, turning once halfway through grilling time.

To Cook by Direct Grill Method: Grill meat on the grill rack of an uncovered grill directly over *medium* coals for 14 to 18 minutes or till no pink remains, turning once halfway through grilling time.

To Serve: Toast the bread on the grill. In a small saucepan, warm the pizza sauce with the olives. Spoon some of the sauce mixture over toasted bread. Top with patties. Spoon remaining pizza sauce mixture over patties and sprinkle with cheese.

Per serving: 316 calories / 22 g protein / 25 g carbohydrate / 14 g fat (2 g saturated) / 111 mg cholesterol / 863 mg sodium / 504 mg potassium.

Salad Burgers

Indirect Grilling   Serves 4

Meat Mixture:	1	beaten egg
	⅓	cup finely chopped cucumber
	¼	cup toasted wheat germ
	2	tablespoons buttermilk ranch salad dressing *or* creamy cucumber salad dressing
	½	teaspoon garlic salt
	¼	teaspoon dried marjoram, crushed
		Dash pepper
	1	pound lean ground lamb
Bread:	4	kaiser rolls
Toppings:	8	thin cucumber slices
	¼	cup buttermilk ranch salad dressing *or* creamy cucumber salad dressing
	¼	cup alfalfa sprouts

Where's the salad? It's in the burger. You'll find cucumber and buttermilk dressing inside this tasty lamb burger and on top of it, too!

To Prepare Meat Mixture: In a medium mixing bowl combine all meat mixture ingredients *except* lamb. Add ground lamb and mix well. Shape mixture into four ¾-inch-thick patties.

To Cook by Indirect Grill Method: In a covered grill arrange preheated coals around a drip pan. Test for *medium* heat above the pan. Place meat on the grill rack over the drip pan. Cover and grill for 20 to 24 minutes or till no pink remains, turning once halfway through grilling time.

To Serve: Split rolls and toast on the grill. Serve patties in rolls with cucumber slices, salad dressing, and alfalfa sprouts.

Toasting Buns, Rolls, and Bread

A little extra touch, like toasting the bun or bread for a sandwich, makes an already great sandwich even better. Take advantage of your hot grill and leave your kitchen cool, by toasting the buns on the grill.

To grill, place the bun or roll halves or bread, cut side down, on a grill rack directly over the coals. Grill about 1 minute or till lightly toasted.

Per serving: 506 calories / 29 g protein / 35 g carbohydrate / 28 g fat (7 g saturated) / 129 mg cholesterol / 750 mg sodium / 422 mg potassium.

Five-Spice Burgers

Indirect or Direct Grilling   Marinating Time: 1 to 2 hours   Serves 4

Meat Mixture:	1	beaten egg
	¼	cup fine dry bread crumbs
	¼	cup finely shredded carrot
	1	tablespoon milk
	1	clove garlic, minced
	½	teaspoon five-spice powder
	⅛	teaspoon salt
	1	pound lean ground beef
Marinade:	¼	cup teriyaki sauce
Bread:	4	hamburger buns
Toppings:	4	large spinach leaves

Teriyaki sauce and five-spice powder lend the very American burger an Oriental flair.

To Prepare Meat Mixture: In a medium mixing bowl combine all meat mixture ingredients *except* beef. Add ground beef and mix well. Shape mixture into four ¾-inch-thick patties.

To Marinate: Place patties in a shallow baking dish. Pour teriyaki sauce over patties. Cover and refrigerate for 1 to 2 hours, turning once. Remove patties from baking dish and pat dry with paper towels; discard marinade.

To Cook by Indirect Grill Method: In a covered grill arrange preheated coals around a drip pan. Test for *medium* heat above the pan. Place meat on the grill rack over the drip pan. Cover and grill for 20 to 24 minutes or till no pink remains, turning once halfway through grilling time.

To Cook by Direct Grill Method: Grill meat on an uncovered grill directly over *medium* coals for 14 to 18 minutes or till no pink remains, turning once halfway through grilling time.

To Serve: Split the buns and toast on the grill. Serve patties in buns with spinach.

Per serving: 348 calories / 27 g protein / 26 g carbohydrate / 14 g fat (5 g saturated) / 125 mg cholesterol / 571 mg sodium / 317 mg potassium.

Ham Mini-Loaves

Indirect or Direct Grilling

Serves 4

Meat Mixture:		
	1	beaten egg
	¾	cup soft bread crumbs (1 slice)
	2	tablespoons milk
	2	tablespoons finely chopped onion
	1	teaspoon prepared horseradish
	8	ounces lean ground pork
	8	ounces ground fully cooked ham
Sauce:	¼	cup currant jelly
	3	tablespoons catsup
	1	teaspoon prepared mustard
	1	teaspoon Worcestershire sauce
Garnish:	2	cups finely shredded lettuce

Any loaves leftover? Serve 'em like cold meat loaf sandwiches. Put a mini-loaf on a slice of bread, drizzle with sauce, sprinkle on lettuce, and top it off with another piece of bread.

To Prepare Meat Mixture: In a medium mixing bowl combine all meat mixture ingredients *except* pork and ham. Add pork and ham and mix well. Shape mixture into 4 mini loaves, each about 4x2½x¾ inches in size. Set aside.

For Sauce: In a small saucepan combine all sauce ingredients. Cook and stir just till boiling. Remove from heat; cover and keep warm while grilling meat.

To Cook by Indirect Grill Method: In a covered grill arrange preheated coals around a drip pan. Test for *medium* heat above the pan. Place meat on the grill rack over the drip pan. Cover and grill for 20 to 24 minutes or till juices run clear, turning once halfway through grilling time.

To Cook by Direct Grill Method: Grill meat on the grill rack of an uncovered grill directly over *medium* coals for 14 to 18 minutes or till juices run clear, turning once halfway through grilling time.

To Serve: Place ½ *cup* lettuce on *each* plate and top with meat patties. Spoon sauce over the patties.

Per serving: 259 calories / 22 g protein / 22 g carbohydrate / 9 g fat (1 g saturated) / 97 mg cholesterol / 909 mg sodium / 464 mg potassium.

Ham Mini-Loaves

Chimichanga-Style Beef Bundles

Indirect or Direct Grilling   Serves 6

Tortillas:	6 10-inch flour tortillas
Meat Mixture:	1 pound lean ground beef
	½ cup chopped onion (1 medium)
	1 clove garlic, minced
	1 large tomato, peeled, seeded, and chopped
	1 4-ounce can diced green chili peppers, drained
	¼ teaspoon salt
	¼ teaspoon ground cumin
	Several dashes bottled hot pepper sauce
	2 cups shredded Monterey Jack cheese (8 ounces)
Toppings:	1 6-ounce container frozen avocado dip, thawed *or* 1 cup salsa
Garnish:	Fresh cilantro (optional)

There's no deep-fat frying needed to get the tortilla shells crisp and crunchy— that's what the grilling does.

For Tortillas: Wrap the tortillas in foil and heat in a 350° oven for 10 minutes to soften.

To Prepare Meat Mixture: Meanwhile, in a large skillet cook beef, onion, and garlic till meat is brown and onion is tender. Drain off fat. Stir in tomato, chili peppers, salt, cumin, and hot pepper sauce. Remove one tortilla at a time from foil packet and spoon about ½ *cup* of the meat mixture just below the center of the tortilla. Sprinkle with ⅓ *cup* of the cheese. Fold bottom edge of tortilla up and over filling, just till mixture is covered. Fold opposite sides of tortilla in, just till they meet. Roll filled section over onto opposite edge of tortilla. If necessary, secure with wooden toothpicks. Repeat with remaining tortillas, meat, and cheese.

To Cook by Indirect Grill Method: In a covered grill arrange preheated coals around a drip pan. Test for *medium-low* heat above the pan. Place packets, seam side down, on the grill rack over the drip pan. Cover and grill for 20 to 25 minutes or till heated through.

To Cook by Direct Grill Method: Place packets, seam side down, on the grill rack of an uncovered grill directly over *medium-low* coals for 15 to 20 minutes or till heated through, turning once halfway through grilling time.

To Serve: Top each packet with avocado dip or salsa. If desired, garnish with sprigs of cilantro.

Per serving: 431 calories / 27 g protein / 30 g carbohydrate / 22 g fat (10 g saturated) / 81 mg cholesterol / 411 mg sodium / 260 mg potassium.

Sesame Pork Ribs

| Indirect Grilling | Marinating Time: 6 to 24 hour | Serves 4 |

Marinade:	¼ cup water
	¼ cup soy sauce
	¼ cup dry sherry
Meat:	2 to 2½ pounds pork country-style ribs
Sauce:	¼ cup soy sauce
	¼ cup dry sherry
	1 tablespoon sugar
	1 tablespoon lemon juice
	2 teaspoons sesame seed, toasted and crushed
	1 teaspoon grated gingerroot *or* ¼ teaspoon ground ginger
	1 teaspoon toasted sesame oil

Ginger and sesame—two terrific tastes make for one great rib recipe.

For Marinade: In a small mixing bowl combine all marinade ingredients.

To Prepare Ribs: Place ribs in a plastic bag set into a deep bowl. Pour marinade over ribs in bag. Seal bag and turn ribs to coat well. Marinate in the refrigerator for 6 to 24 hours, turning bag occasionally. Remove ribs from bag; discard marinade.

For Sauce: In a small mixing bowl combine all sauce ingredients. Set aside.

To Cook by Indirect Grill Method: In a covered grill arrange preheated coals around a drip pan. Test for *medium* heat above the pan. Place ribs on the grill rack over the drip pan. Cover and grill for 1½ to 2 hours or till ribs are tender and no pink remains, brushing occasionally with the sauce.

Per serving: 463 calories / 39 g protein / 7 g carbohydrate / 28 g fat (9 g saturated) / 145 mg cholesterol / 1,159 mg sodium / 610 mg potassium.

Spiced-and-Smoked Ribs

Indirect Grilling   Serves 6

Wood Chips:	4	cups hickory chips
Meat:	4	pounds meaty pork spareribs *or* pork loin back ribs
Seasoning Rub:	1	tablespoon brown sugar
	1	teaspoon five-spice powder
	½	teaspoon paprika
	¼	teaspoon salt
	¼	teaspoon celery seed
	¼	teaspoon pepper
Glaze:	½	cup catsup
	2	tablespoons light molasses
	1	tablespoon lemon juice
	1	tablespoon soy sauce
		Several dashes bottled hot pepper sauce

First, coat the ribs with a spice rub. Then slather them with the molasses glaze while you grill.

To Prepare Wood Chips: At least 1 hour before grilling, soak wood chips in enough water to cover. Drain chips before using.

To Precook Ribs: Cut ribs into serving-size pieces. Place ribs in a Dutch oven. Add enough water to cover ribs. Bring to boiling; reduce heat. Cover and simmer for 30 minutes. Drain ribs; cool ribs slightly.

For Seasoning Rub: In a small mixing bowl combine all seasoning rub ingredients. When ribs are cool enough to handle, rub seasoning mixture over ribs.

For Glaze: In a small mixing bowl combine all glaze ingredients. Set aside.

To Cook by Indirect Grill Method: In a covered grill arrange preheated coals around a drip pan. Test for *medium* heat above the pan. Sprinkle the drained wood chips onto the preheated coals. Place precooked ribs on the grill rack over the drip pan. Cover and grill for 45 to 50 minutes or till ribs are tender and no pink remains, brushing occasionally with the glaze the last 15 minutes of grilling.

Per serving: 520 calories / 35 g protein / 13 g carbohydrate / 36 g fat (14 g saturated) / 143 mg cholesterol / 610 mg sodium / 562 mg potassium.

Spiced and Smoked Ribs

Pineapple-Sauced Country-Style Pork Ribs

Indirect Grilling   Serves 4

Sauce:	⅓ cup frozen pineapple juice concentrate, thawed
	3 tablespoons Dijon-style mustard
Meat:	2½ to 3 pounds pork country-style ribs

It's hard to believe that a sauce so yummy contains only two ingredients.

For Sauce: In a small bowl combine pineapple juice concentrate and mustard. Set aside.

To Prepare Meat: Trim fat from meat.

To Cook by Indirect Grill Method: In a covered grill arrange preheated coals around a drip pan. Test for *medium* heat above the pan.

Place ribs on the grill rack over the drip pan. Cover and grill for 1½ to 2 hours or till ribs are tender and no pink remains, brushing occasionally with the sauce the last 15 minutes of grilling.

Per serving: 541 calories / 41 g protein / 11 g carbohydrate / 35 g fat (12 g saturated) / 162 mg cholesterol / 408 mg sodium / 789 mg potassium.

Peanut-Sauced Ribs

Indirect Grilling   Serves 6

Sauce:	3 tablespoons hot water
	⅓ cup peanut butter
	½ of a 6-ounce can (⅓ cup) apple juice concentrate, thawed
	3 tablespoons cooking oil
	2 tablespoons teriyaki sauce
	1 tablespoon curry powder
	2 cloves garlic, minced
	Several dashes bottled hot pepper sauce
Meat:	4 pounds pork loin back ribs *or* meaty spareribs

Peanut butter, apple juice concentrate, teriyaki sauce, and curry powder are the secrets to the spicy, Indian-inspired brushing sauce.

For Sauce: In a small mixing bowl gradually stir hot water into peanut butter. (The mixture will stiffen at first.) Stir in remaining sauce ingredients till mixture is smooth. Set sauce aside.

To Prepare Meat: Cut the ribs into serving-size pieces.

To Cook by Indirect Grill Method: In a covered grill arrange preheated coals around a drip pan. Test for *medium* heat above the pan. Place ribs on the grill rack over the drip pan. Cover and grill for 1¼ to 1½ hours or till ribs are tender and no pink remains, brushing occasionally with sauce the last 10 minutes of grilling. Pass any remaining sauce.

Per serving: 647 calories / 38 g protein / 11 g carbohydrate / 50 g fat (16 g saturated) / 143 mg cholesterol / 413 mg sodium / 583 mg potassium.

Peach-Glazed Baby Back Ribs

Indirect Grilling   Serves 4

Glaze:	1 10-ounce jar peach preserves
	2 tablespoons lemon juice
	1 teaspoon Dijon-style mustard
	¼ teaspoon ground cardamom *or* ground cinnamon
Meat:	4 to 5 pounds pork loin back ribs *or* meaty spareribs

To turn baby back ribs into a glistening showstopper, simply stir together this four ingredient glaze and brush it on toward the end of the slow cooking.

For Glaze: In a small saucepan combine all glaze ingredients. Cook and stir over medium heat till preserves melt. Remove from heat; set aside.

To Prepare Meat: Cut the ribs into serving-size pieces. Sprinkle ribs with *salt* and *pepper*.

To Cook by Indirect Grill Method: In a covered grill arrange preheated coals around a drip pan. Test for *medium* heat above the pan. Place ribs on the grill rack over the drip pan. Cover and grill for 1¼ to 1½ hours or till ribs are tender and no pink remains, brushing with sauce the last 15 minutes of grilling. Pass any additional sauce.

Per serving: 601 calories / 34 g protein / 34 g carbohydrate / 36 g fat (14 g saturated) / 148 mg cholesterol / 223 mg sodium / 429 mg potassium.

Peach-Glazed Baby Back Ribs

Barbecued Beef Ribs

Indirect Grilling   Serves 6

Meat:	3 to 4 pounds beef chuck short ribs with bone *or* 2 to 2½ pounds without bone
Sauce:	1 8-ounce can tomato sauce
	¼ cup water
	2 tablespoons brown sugar
	2 tablespoons vinegar *or* lemon juice
	1 tablespoon Worcestershire sauce
	1 tablespoon finely chopped onion
	1 teaspoon crushed red pepper

Bring on the barbecue! Here's the kind of blue-ribbon recipe—lusty, yet all-American—that earned a name for barbecue.

To Precook Ribs: Trim fat from meat. Cut ribs into serving-size pieces. Place ribs in a Dutch oven. Add enough water to cover ribs. Bring to boiling; reduce heat. Cover and simmer about 2 hours or till meat is tender. Drain ribs.

For Sauce: Meanwhile, in a small saucepan combine all sauce ingredients. Bring to boiling; reduce heat. Simmer, uncovered, for 10 minutes, stirring once or twice. Remove from heat.

To Cook by Indirect Grill Method: In a covered grill arrange preheated coals around a drip pan. Test for *medium* heat above the pan. Place precooked ribs on the grill rack over the drip pan. Brush with the sauce. Cover and grill for 15 minutes, brushing occasionally with the sauce.

Per serving: 510 calories / 33 g protein / 8 g carbohydrate / 19 g fat (8 g saturated) / 97 mg cholesterol / 338 mg sodium / 523 mg potassium.

Sweetly Spiced Roast Pork

Indirect Grilling   Serves 8

Seasoning Rub:	¼ cup packed brown sugar
	2 cloves garlic, minced
	1 teaspoon ground ginger
	¼ teaspoon salt
	¼ teaspoon pepper
	⅛ teaspoon ground cinnamon
	Dash ground cloves
Meat:	1 2-pound boneless pork top loin roast (single loin)
	1 tablespoon soy sauce

Accent this succulent roast with new potatoes grilled to perfection (see chart, page 234) and a crisp green salad. Then for dessert, try homemade vanilla ice cream drizzled with caramel sauce and sprinkled with nuts.

For Seasoning Rub: In a small mixing bowl combine all seasoning rub ingredients.

To Prepare Meat: Trim fat from meat. Brush soy sauce over surface of meat. Rub meat with seasoning mixture. Insert a meat thermometer near the center of roast.

To Cook by Indirect Grill Method: In a covered grill arrange preheated coals for indirect cooking. Test for *medium-low* heat where meat will cook. Place meat on a rack in a roasting pan on the grill rack. Cover and grill for 1 to 1¼ hours or till meat thermometer registers 160° to 170°. Slice to serve.

Pork Update

Today's pork is leaner and lower in fat and calories than ever before. And because there is so little fat, it is essential to carefully watch the time and temperature in each recipe to ensure that you serve flavorful, tender, juicy meat.

To achieve the best flavor, the latest recommendations for cooking pork now offer a choice of doneness for selected pork cuts. Roasts and chops from the loin and rib sections can be cooked to an internal temperature of 160° (medium well) or 170° (well done). The meat will be slightly pink at 160°, but when a small cut is made in the meat, the juices should run clear.

Ground pork and the less-tender cuts of pork, such as sirloin or loin blade roasts and chops, should be cooked to 170° (well done) or till no pink remains.

Per serving: 164 calories / 16 g protein / 7 g carbohydrate / 7 g fat (3 g saturated) / 51 mg cholesterol / 237 mg sodium / 238 mg potassium.

Rhubarb-Glazed Pork Roast

Indirect Grilling   Serves 4

Glaze:	6 ounces fresh *or* frozen rhubarb, sliced (about 1 cup)
	½ of a 6-ounce can (⅓ cup) frozen apple juice concentrate
	Few drops red food coloring (optional)
	1 tablespoon honey
Meat:	1 2-pound pork loin center rib roast with backbone loosened

Once you see the glistening ruby glaze and taste the juicy pork, you'll know why this is a favorite recipe of many editors.

For Glaze: In a small saucepan combine rhubarb, juice concentrate, and if desired, red food coloring. Bring to boiling; reduce heat. Cover and simmer for 15 to 20 minutes or till rhubarb is very tender. Strain, pressing liquid out of pulp. Discard pulp. Return liquid to the saucepan. Bring to boiling; reduce heat. Simmer, uncovered, for 10 to 15 minutes or till rhubarb liquid is reduced to ¼ cup. Remove from heat. Stir in honey.

To Prepare Meat: Trim fat from meat. Insert a meat thermometer near the center of the roast not touching bone.

To Cook by Indirect Grill Method: In a covered grill arrange preheated coals for indirect cooking. Test for *medium* heat where meat will cook. Place meat on a rack in a roasting pan on the grill rack. Cover and grill for 1½ to 2 hours or till meat thermometer registers 160° to 170°, brushing occasionally with glaze after 1¼ hours. Slice to serve.

Per serving: 268 calories / 24 g protein / 17 g carbohydrate / 11 g fat (4 g saturated) / 75 mg cholesterol / 66 mg sodium / 544 mg potassium.

South-of-the-Border Pork Tenderloin

Indirect Grilling   Serves 6

Meat:	2	12-ounce pork tenderloins
	¾	cup shredded Monterey Jack cheese with jalapeño peppers (3 ounces)
Stuffing:	¼	cup chopped onion
	1	tablespoon margarine *or* butter
	1	cup corn bread stuffing mix
	3	tablespoons pine nuts *or* slivered almonds, chopped
	2	tablespoons water
	¼	teaspoon ground cumin
		Cooking oil
Sauce:	1	cup salsa (optional)

The Monterey Jack cheese with jalapeño peppers gives the stuffing a real kick. For a milder version, use plain Monterey Jack cheese.

To Prepare Meat: Split both tenderloins lengthwise, cutting to but not through the opposite side. Spread meat open. Overlap one long side of each tenderloin about 2 inches. Place pork between 2 pieces of plastic wrap. Working from the center to the edges, pound lightly with the flat side of a meat mallet to form a 10-inch square, about ⅛ to ¼ inch thick. Remove plastic wrap. Sprinkle cheese over the meat to within 1 inch of edge.

For Stuffing: In a saucepan cook onion in margarine or butter till onion is tender but not brown. Remove from heat. Stir in stuffing mix, pine nuts or almonds, water, and cumin; mix well. Spoon filling over the cheese to within 1 inch of edge of meat. Fold bottom edge over stuffing and fold in the sides. Starting at one end with seam, roll up jelly-roll style. Tie with string at 1-inch intervals. Brush all surfaces of meat with a little cooking oil.

To Cook by Indirect Grill Method: In a covered grill arrange preheated coals for indirect cooking. Test for *medium* heat where meat will cook. Place meat on a rack in a roasting pan on the grill rack. Cover and grill about 1½ hours or till juices run clear, occasionally brushing meat with cooking oil. Remove strings. Slice meat; if desired, serve with salsa.

Per serving: 303 calories / 30 g protein / 5 g carbohydrate / 18 g fat (6 g saturated) / 93 mg cholesterol / 243 mg sodium / 540 mg potassium.

Marinated Leg of Lamb

Indirect Grilling   Marinating Time: 6 to 24 hours   Serves 16

Marinade:	
	½ cup cooking oil
	⅓ cup lemon juice
	¼ cup finely chopped onion
	2 tablespoons snipped parsley
	1 teaspoon salt
	½ teaspoon dried thyme, crushed
	½ teaspoon dried basil, crushed
	¼ teaspoon dried tarragon, crushed
Meat:	1 4-pound boneless leg of lamb, rolled and tied

For a more intense flavor from the marinade, untie the meat before marinating and reroll and tie before grilling.

For Marinade: In a small mixing bowl combine all marinade ingredients.

To Prepare Meat: Trim fat from meat. Place meat in a plastic bag set into a shallow dish. Pour marinade over meat in bag. Seal bag and turn meat to coat well. Marinate in the refrigerator for 6 to 24 hours, turning bag occasionally. Remove meat from bag, reserving marinade. Chill marinade while grilling meat. Insert meat thermometer near the center of roast.

To Cook by Indirect Grill Method: In a covered grill arrange preheated coals for indirect cooking. Test for *medium-low* where meat will cook. Place meat on a rack in a roasting pan on the grill rack. Cover and grill for 2¼ to 3 hours or till meat thermometer registers 140° (rare) to 160° (medium-well), brushing occasionally with reserved marinade during the first 2 hours. Remove strings and slice meat to serve.

Per serving: 214 calories / 18 g protein / 0 g carbohydrate / 15 g fat (5 g saturated) / 66 mg cholesterol / 114 mg sodium / 230 mg potassium.

Herbed Chuck Roast

Indirect Grilling	Marinating Time. 6 to 24 hours	Serves 10

Marinade:	1 cup vinegar
	1 cup water
	2 medium onions, sliced
	½ lemon, sliced
	2 tablespoons snipped fresh rosemary *or* 2 teaspoons dried rosemary, crushed
	1 teaspoon salt
	1 teaspoon cracked pepper
Meat:	1 3- to 4-pound beef chuck pot roast, cut 2 inches thick

For a summertime version of a wintertime favorite, pot roast and potatoes, serve this flavorful roast along with the Grilled Vegetable Packet (see recipe, page 175).

For Marinade: In a medium mixing bowl combine all marinade ingredients.

To Prepare Meat: Trim fat from meat. Place meat in a plastic bag set into a deep bowl. Pour marinade over meat in bag. Seal bag and turn meat to coat well. Marinate in the refrigerator for 6 to 24 hours, turning bag occasionally. Remove meat from bag; discard the marinade.

To Cook by Indirect Grill Method: In a covered grill arrange preheated coals for indirect cooking. Test for *medium-low* heat where meat will cook. Place meat on a rack in a roasting pan on the grill rack. Cover and grill to desired doneness (see chart).

Indirect Grilling

Doneness	Internal Temp.	Hours
Rare	(140°)	1
Medium	(160°)	1 hour and 25 minutes

Per serving: 228 calories / 32 g protein / 1 g carbohydrate / 10 g fat (4 g saturated) / 99 mg cholesterol / 118 mg sodium / 297 mg potassium.

Sweet-Onion-Marinated Beef Eye Roast

Sweet-Onion-Marinated Beef Eye Roast

Indirect Grilling   Marinating Time: 6 to 24 hours   Serves 12

Marinade:
- ½ cup dry white wine
- ¼ cup olive oil *or* cooking oil
- 2 teaspoons coarsely ground pepper
- 2 teaspoons dried dillweed
- ½ teaspoon salt

Meat:
- 1 2- to 3-pound beef eye of round roast
- 2 medium onions

Sauce:
- ⅔ cup mayonnaise *or* salad dressing
- ⅓ cup dairy sour cream
- 2 tablespoons prepared horseradish
- 1 teaspoon dried dillweed
- ⅛ teaspoon salt
- ⅛ teaspoon pepper

For a sweeter-tasting simmered onion mixture, start with sweet onions such as Vidalia onions.

For Marinade: In a small mixing bowl combine all marinade ingredients.

To Prepare Meat: Trim fat from meat. Thinly slice onions and separate into rings. Place meat and onions in a plastic bag set into a shallow dish. Pour marinade over meat in bag. Seal bag and turn meat to coat well. Marinate in the refrigerator for 6 to 24 hours, turning bag occasionally. Remove meat from bag, reserving marinade and onions. Chill marinade and onions while grilling meat. Insert meat thermometer near the center of the roast.

To Cook by Indirect Grill Method: In a covered grill arrange preheated coals for indirect cooking. Test for *medium-low* heat where meat will cook. Place meat on a rack in a roasting pan on the grill rack. Cover and grill to desired doneness (see chart).

Indirect Grilling

Doneness	Internal Temp.	Hours
Rare	(140°)	1 to 1½
Medium	(160°)	1½ to 2

For Sauce: Meanwhile, in a small mixing bowl stir together all sauce ingredients. Cover and chill till serving time.

To Serve: In a large skillet bring reserved onions and marinade to boiling; reduce heat. Cover and simmer about 12 minutes or till onions are tender. Thinly slice the roast and serve hot with the simmered onion mixture and sauce.

Per serving: 297 calories / 24 g protein / 2 g carbohydrate / 20 g fat (5 g saturated) / 66 mg cholesterol / 263 mg sodium / 380 mg potassium.

Peppered Chutney Roast

Indirect Grilling	Marinating Time: 6 to 24 hours	Serves 10

Marinade:	¾ cup unsweetened pineapple juice
	½ cup steak sauce
	⅓ cup orange juice
	¼ cup lemon juice
	¼ cup Worcestershire sauce
	1 tablespoon sugar
	1 teaspoon seasoned salt
	1 teaspoon lemon-pepper seasoning
Meat:	1 2½- to 3-pound beef tenderloin
	1½ teaspoons cracked pepper
	¼ cup chutney, snipped

Wow, what a marinade! Don't stop with the tenderloin, give the marinade a try with other cuts of beef, pork, chicken, or turkey, too.

For Marinade: In a small mixing bowl combine all marinade ingredients.

To Prepare Meat: Place meat in a plastic bag set into a shallow dish. Pour marinade over meat in bag. Seal bag and turn meat to coat well. Marinate in the refrigerator for 6 to 24 hours, turning bag occasionally. Remove meat from bag, reserving marinade. Chill marinade while grilling meat. Rub meat with the cracked pepper. Insert meat thermometer near the center of roast.

To Cook by Indirect Grill Method: In a covered grill arrange preheated coals for indirect cooking. Test for *medium-high* heat where meat will cook. Place meat on a rack in a roasting pan on the grill rack. Cover and grill for 35 to 45 minutes or till meat thermometer registers 135°, brushing with reserved marinade halfway through grilling time. Spoon chutney evenly over the meat. Cover and grill meat till thermometer registers 140° (rare). Slice to serve.

Per serving: 178 calories / 22 g protein / 6 g carbohydrate / 7 g fat (3 g saturated) / 64 mg cholesterol / 132 mg sodium / 347 mg potassium.

Grilled Rump Roast

Indirect Grilling

Meat:	1 3-pound boneless beef round rump roast
Sauce:	½ cup catsup
	½ cup water
	¼ cup vinegar
	½ envelope (2 tablespoons) regular onion soup mix
	2 tablespoons sugar
	2 tablespoons cooking oil
	1 tablespoon prepared mustard

For casual fare, turn this knife-and-fork entree into bun-bursting sandwiches. It's easy—slice the meat thin, pile it high on fresh onion buns, and top it with sauce.

To Prepare Meat: Trim fat from meat. Insert a meat thermometer near the center of roast.

To Cook by Indirect Grill Method: In a covered grill arrange preheated coals for indirect cooking. Test for *medium-low* heat where meat will cook. Place meat on a rack in a roasting pan on the grill rack. Cover and grill to desired doneness (see chart).

Indirect Grilling

Doneness	Internal Temp.	Hours
Rare	(140°)	1¼ to 1½
Medium	(160°)	1½ to 2

For Sauce: In a medium saucepan combine all ingredients. Bring to boiling; reduce heat. Simmer, uncovered, for 5 minutes. Slice meat and pass sauce.

Per serving: 333 calories / 39 g protein / 9 g carbohydrate / 15 g fat (5 g saturated) / 116 mg cholesterol / 471 mg sodium / 468 mg potassium.

Cajun-Style Pork Chops

Indirect or Direct Grilling   Serves 4

Seasoning Rub:	1 teaspoon onion powder
	¼ to ½ teaspoon ground white pepper
	¼ to ½ teaspoon ground red pepper
	¼ to ½ teaspoon pepper
	¼ teaspoon salt
Meat:	4 pork loin *or* rib chops, cut 1¼ inches thick (about 2¼ pounds total)

Make sure there's a tall glass of water nearby when you bite into these peppery chops.

For Seasoning Rub: In a small mixing bowl combine all seasoning rub ingredients.

To Prepare Meat: Trim fat from meat. Rub both sides of each pork chop with the seasoning rub.

To Cook by Indirect Grill Method: In a covered grill arrange preheated coals around a drip pan. Test for *medium* heat above the pan.

Place pork chops on the grill rack over the drip pan. Cover and grill for 35 to 45 minutes or till juices run clear, turning once.

To Cook by Direct Grill Method: Grill pork chops on the grill rack of an uncovered grill directly over *medium* coals for 25 to 35 minutes or till juices run clear, turning once.

Per serving: 207 calories / 24 g protein / 1 g carbohydrate / 11 g fat (4 g saturated) / 77 mg cholesterol / 192 mg sodium / 319 mg potassium.

Oriental Pork Chops

Indirect Grilling　　　　　　　　Marinating Time: 6 to 24 hours　　　　　　Serves 4

Marinade:	⅓	cup soy sauce
	¼	cup cooking oil
	1	tablespoon finely shredded orange peel
	¼	cup orange juice
	¼	cup finely chopped green pepper
	1	tablespoon brown sugar
	2	teaspoons ground ginger
	1	teaspoon ground turmeric
Meat:	4	pork loin *or* rib chops, cut 1¼ inches thick (about 2¼ pounds total)
Wood Chips:	4	cups hickory wood chips *or* mesquite wood chips (optional)

Super easy and simply sensational. Marinate the chops one night, and grill them the next.

For Marinade: In a small mixing bowl combine all of the marinade ingredients.

To Prepare Meat: Trim fat from meat. Place pork chops in a plastic bag set into a deep bowl. Pour marinade over chops in bag. Seal bag and turn chops to coat well. Marinate in the refrigerator for 6 to 24 hours, turning bag occasionally. Remove chops from bag, reserving marinade. Chill marinade while grilling meat.

To Prepare Wood Chips: If using, at least 1 hour before grilling, soak wood chips in enough water to cover. Drain the chips before using.

To Cook by Indirect Grill Method: In a covered grill arrange preheated coals around a drip pan. Test for *medium* heat above the pan. If using, sprinkle *1 cup* of the drained wood chips onto the preheated coals. Place pork chops on the grill rack over the drip pan. Cover and grill for 35 to 50 minutes or till juices run clear, turning once and brushing with reserved marinade after 25 minutes. Add additional drained wood chips, if using, as necessary.

Per serving: 466 calories / 38 g protein / 9 g carbohydrate / 30 g fat (8 g saturated) / 116 mg cholesterol / 1,448 mg sodium / 588 mg potassium.

Blue-Cheese-Stuffed Pork Chops

Blue-Cheese-Stuffed Pork Chops

Indirect Grilling   Serves 4

Stuffing:	½ cup shredded carrot
	¼ cup chopped pecans
	¼ cup crumbled blue cheese
	1 green onion, thinly sliced
	1 teaspoon Worcestershire sauce
Meat:	4 pork loin *or* rib chops, cut 1¼ inches thick (about 2¼ pounds total)
Sauce:	¼ cup plain yogurt
	4 teaspoons all-purpose flour
	¾ cup milk
	½ teaspoon instant chicken bouillon granules
	Dash pepper

For true blue cheese fans, sprinkle additional blue cheese and chopped pecans over the sauce-covered pork chops.

For Stuffing: In a small mixing bowl combine all stuffing ingredients.

To Prepare Meat: Trim fat from meat. Make a pocket in each chop by cutting horizontally into the chop from the fat side almost to the bone. Spoon about ¼ *cup* of the stuffing into *each* pocket. If necessary, securely fasten the opening with wooden toothpicks.

To Cook by Indirect Grill Method: In a covered grill arrange preheated coals around a drip pan. Test for *medium* heat above the pan. Place chops on the grill rack over the drip pan. Cover and grill for 30 to 40 minutes or till juices run clear.

For Sauce: In a small saucepan stir together the yogurt and flour. Add remaining sauce ingredients. Cook and stir till thickened and bubbly. Cook and stir for 2 minutes more.

To Serve: Remove toothpicks from chops and serve sauce over chops.

Per serving: 420 calories / 41 g protein / 7 g carbohydrate / 24 g fat (8 g saturated) / 126 mg cholesterol / 332 mg sodium / 665 mg potassium.

Veal Chops with Apples

Indirect or Direct Grilling	Marinating Time: 6 to 24 hours	Serves 4

Marinade:	¼ cup dry white wine
	2 tablespoons snipped fresh sage *or* 1 teaspoon dried sage, crushed
	2 tablespoons cooking oil
	¼ teaspoon salt
	¼ teaspoon pepper
Meat:	4 boneless veal top loin chops, cut ¾ inch thick (about 1 pound total)
Fruit:	2 medium tart cooking apples

Some autumn afternoon make a trip to the orchard or market and buy some fresh-from-the-tree tart cooking apples (such as Granny Smiths, Jonathans, McIntosh, or Empires) to grill along with this mildly marinated veal.

For Marinade: In a small mixing bowl combine all marinade ingredients.

To Prepare Meat: Trim fat from meat. Place veal chops in a plastic bag set into a deep bowl. Pour marinade over chops in bag. Seal bag and turn chops to coat well. Marinate in the refrigerator for 6 to 24 hours, turning bag occasionally.

To Prepare Fruit: Just before grilling, remove cores from apples. Cut crosswise into 1-inch-thick slices; set aside.

To Cook by Indirect Grill Method: Remove chops from bag, reserving marinade. In a small saucepan bring marinade to boiling; reduce heat. Simmer, uncovered, for 1 minute. In a covered grill arrange preheated coals around a drip pan. Test for *medium* heat above the pan. Place veal chops and apple slices on the grill rack over the drip pan. Cover and grill for 14 to 18 minutes or till veal and apples are tender and meat juices run clear, brushing occasionally with reserved marinade during the first 8 minutes of grilling. Serve chops with apple slices.

To Cook by Direct Grill Method: Remove chops from bag, reserving marinade. In a small saucepan bring marinade to boiling; reduce heat. Simmer, uncovered, for 1 minute. Grill veal chops and apple slices on the grill rack of an uncovered grill directly over *medium* coals for 11 to 13 minutes or till veal and apples are tender and meat juices run clear, turning chops and apples once halfway through grilling time and brushing with reserved marinade. Serve chops with apple slices.

Per serving: 240 calories / 19 g protein / 11 g carbohydrate / 12 g fat (3 g saturated) / 77 mg cholesterol / 205 mg sodium / 350 mg potassium.

Minted-and-Marinated Lamb Chops

	Indirect or Direct Grilling	Marinating Time: 6 to 24 hours	Serves 4
Marinade:	3 tablespoons cooking oil		
	2 tablespoons lemon juice		
	1 tablespoon snipped fresh mint *or* 1 teaspoon dried mint, crushed		
	1 tablespoon water		
	2 cloves garlic, minced		
	½ teaspoon seasoned salt		
	¼ teaspoon pepper		
Meat:	8 lamb rib *or* loin chops *or* 4 leg sirloin chops, cut 1 inch thick (about 2½ pounds total)		

Make the lamb chops look company special. Dollop them with yogurt and garnish with a fresh sprig of mint.

For Marinade: In a small mixing bowl combine all marinade ingredients.

To Prepare Meat: Trim fat from meat. Place lamb chops in a plastic bag set into a deep bowl. Pour marinade over chops in bag. Seal bag and turn chops to coat well. Marinate in the refrigerator for 6 to 24 hours, turning bag occasionally. Remove chops from bag, reserving marinade.

To Cook by Indirect Grill Method: In a covered grill arrange preheated coals around a drip pan. Test for *medium* heat above the pan. Place lamb chops on the grill rack over the drip pan. Cover and grill for 16 to 20 minutes or till desired doneness, turning chops once and brushing with reserved marinade halfway through grilling time.

To Cook by Direct Grill Method: Grill lamb chops on the grill rack of an uncovered grill directly over *medium* coals for 10 to 16 minutes or till desired doneness, turning chops once and brushing with reserved marinade halfway through grilling time.

Per serving: 291 calories / 34 g protein / 1 g carbohydrate / 16 g fat (5 g saturated) / 111 mg cholesterol / 243 mg sodium / 359 mg potassium.

Lamb Chops with Rosemary

Indirect or Direct Grilling   Serves 4

Marinade:	⅓ cup dry white wine
	⅓ cup lemon juice
	¼ cup finely chopped onion
	3 tablespoons olive oil *or* cooking oil
	1 tablespoon snipped fresh rosemary *or* 1 teaspoon dried rosemary, crushed
	½ teaspoon salt
	¼ teaspoon pepper
Meat:	8 lamb loin chops, cut 1 inch thick (about 2½ pounds total)
Garnish	Fresh rosemary sprigs (optional)

Make any occasion special with a dinner of fresh, delicately seasoned lamb chops, baked potatoes, steamed beans topped with chopped tomatoes, and white wine.

For Marinade: In a small mixing bowl combine all the marinade ingredients.

To Prepare Meat: Trim fat from meat. Place lamb chops in a plastic bag set into a deep bowl. Pour marinade over chops in bag. Seal bag and turn chops to coat well. Marinate in the refrigerator for 6 to 24 hours, turning bag occasionally. Remove chops from bag, reserving marinade.

To Cook by Indirect Grill Method: In a covered grill arrange preheated coals around a drip pan. Test for *medium* heat above the pan. Place lamb chops on the grill rack over the drip pan. Cover and grill for 16 to 20 minutes or till desired doneness, brushing with reserved marinade halfway through grilling time.

To Cook by Direct Grill Method: Grill lamb chops on the grill rack of an uncovered grill directly over *medium* coals for 10 to 16 minutes or till desired doneness, turning chops once and brushing with reserved marinade halfway through grilling time.

To Serve: If desired, garnish with fresh rosemary.

Per serving: 455 calories / 45 g protein / 3 g carbohydrate / 27 g fat (8 g saturated) / 148 mg cholesterol / 380 mg sodium / 514 mg potassium.

Lamb Chops with Rosemary

Steak with Blue Cheese Butter

Indirect or Direct Grilling · Serves 4

Blue Cheese Butter:	½ cup butter *or* margarine, softened
	½ cup crumbled blue cheese (2 ounces)
	1 tablespoon snipped parsley
	1 teaspoon dried basil, crushed
	1 clove garlic, minced
Meat:	2 1-pound beef porterhouse *or* T-bone steaks, cut 1½ inches thick

This recipe makes more blue cheese butter than you'll need for the steak. Cover and chill the extra butter and serve it over vegetables at your next meal.

For Blue Cheese Butter: In a small mixing bowl stir together butter or margarine, blue cheese, parsley, basil, and garlic. Set aside.

To Prepare Meat: Trim fat from meat.

To Cook by Indirect Grill Method: In a covered grill arrange preheated coals around a drip pan. Test for *medium* heat above the pan. Place meat on the grill rack over the drip pan. Cover and grill to desired doneness (see chart), turning once. Sprinkle steaks with *salt* and *pepper*.

To Cook by Direct Grill Method: Grill steaks on the grill rack of an uncovered grill directly over *medium* coals to desired doneness (see chart), turning once. Sprinkle steaks with *salt* and *pepper*.

Doneness	Indirect	Direct
Rare	20 to 22 minutes	14 to 18 minutes
Medium	22 to 26 minutes	18 to 22 minutes

To Serve: Cut steaks into serving size pieces. Dollop steaks with blue cheese butter.

Steak Doneness

How red is rare and done is done? Take the guess work out of cooking steaks. Use the doneness descriptions below and you'll find that cooking a steak to the doneness of your choice is as easy as that!

Rare steak is red in the center and pink on the edges.

Medium steak still has a little pink in the center, but the edges are gray to brown.

Well-done steak is completely cooked all the way through with no pink remaining.

If you prefer medium-rare doneness, cook your steaks till they look halfway between rare and medium. For medium-well doneness, cook till the steaks appear halfway between medium and well-done.

Mushroom-Horseradish-Stuffed Steak

Indirect or Direct Grilling   Serves 4

Stuffing:	1½	cups sliced fresh mushrooms
	1	medium onion, chopped (½ cup)
	2	cloves garlic, minced
	1	tablespoon margarine *or* butter
	2	tablespoons prepared horseradish
	¼	teaspoon salt
	⅛	teaspoon pepper
Meat:	4	10-ounce beef top loin steaks, cut 1 inch thick
Sauce:	2	tablespoons margarine *or* butter, melted
	1	tablespoon Worcestershire sauce

Calling all horseradish fans—this steak's for you!

For Stuffing: In a medium saucepan cook mushrooms, onion, and garlic in the 1 tablespoon margarine or butter till tender. Stir in horseradish, salt, and pepper.

To Prepare Meat: Trim fat from meat. Cut a pocket in each steak by cutting from the fat side almost to, but not through, other side. Spoon the stuffing into the steak pockets. Fasten pockets with wooden toothpicks.

For Sauce: In a small mixing bowl combine sauce ingredients.

To Cook by Indirect Grill Method: In a covered grill arrange preheated coals around a drip pan. Test for *medium* heat above the pan. Place meat on the grill rack over the drip pan. Cover and grill to desired doneness (see chart), turning once and brushing with sauce the last 10 minutes of grilling.

To Cook by Direct Grill Method: Grill steaks on the grill rack of an uncovered grill directly over *medium* coals to desired doneness (see chart), turning once and brushing with sauce.

Doneness	Indirect	Direct
Rare	16 to 20 minutes	8 to 12 minutes
Medium	20 to 24 minutes	12 to 15 minutes

Per serving: 487 calories / 56 g protein / 5 g carbohydrate / 26 g fat (8 g saturated) / 150 mg cholesterol / 486 mg sodium / 951 mg potassium.

Beef Rolls with Wine Sauce

Indirect Grilling   Serves 4

Filling:	⅓	cup chopped onion
	1	tablespoon margarine *or* butter
	1	10-ounce package frozen chopped spinach, thawed and well drained
	½	cup shredded carrot
	½	cup shredded Swiss cheese (2 ounces)
	¼	teaspoon pepper
Meat:	1	pound boneless beef top round steak, cut ½ inch thick
Sauce:	¼	cup cold water
	3	tablespoons dry red wine
	1	tablespoon margarine *or* butter
	1	teaspoon cornstarch
	½	teaspoon instant beef bouillon granules
	2	tablespoons snipped parsley

A dinner that's fancy enough for entertaining, but casual enough to eat outdoors.

For Filling: In a medium saucepan cook onion in 1 tablespoon margarine or butter till onion is tender. Stir in spinach, carrot, cheese, and pepper.

To Prepare Meat: Trim fat from meat. Cut beef into 4 pieces. Place *each* piece of beef between 2 pieces of plastic wrap. Working from the center to the edges, pound lightly with the flat side of a meat mallet to form an 8x4-inch rectangle (about ⅛ inch thick). Remove and discard plastic wrap.

Place *one-fourth* of the filling at one end of each beef piece. Fold bottom edge over filling and fold in sides. Roll beef up jelly-roll style. Secure beef with small metal skewers or wooden toothpicks.

To Cook by Indirect Grill Method: In a covered grill arrange preheated coals around a drip pan. Test for *medium* heat above the pan. Place beef rolls on the grill rack over the drip pan. Cover and grill for 30 to 40 minutes or till beef is tender, turning once.

For Sauce: In a small saucepan combine all sauce ingredients *except* parsley. Cook and stir till thickened and bubbly. Cook and stir for 2 minutes more. Stir in parsley. Serve sauce with beef rolls.

Per serving: 312 calories / 34 g protein / 8 g carbohydrate / 15 g fat (5 g saturated) / 85 mg cholesterol / 332 mg sodium / 702 mg potassium.

Tropical Fiesta Steak

Indirect or Direct Grilling   Marinating Time: 6 to 24 hours   Serves 6

Marinade:
⅓	cup frozen orange juice concentrate, thawed
3	tablespoons cooking oil
3	tablespoons honey
1	tablespoon sliced green onion
2	teaspoons spicy brown mustard *or* Dijon-style mustard
1	teaspoon snipped fresh mint *or* ¼ teaspoon dried mint, crushed
	Few drops bottled hot pepper sauce

Meat:
1	1½-pound boneless beef sirloin steak (cut 1 inch thick)

Relish:
½	cup chopped red sweet pepper
½	cup chopped red apple
½	cup chopped pear
½	cup chopped, peeled peach
¼	cup chopped celery
1	green onion, sliced (2 tablespoons)
2	teaspoons lemon juice

Sauce:
1	8-ounce carton pineapple yogurt
2	tablespoons milk
1	teaspoon spicy brown mustard *or* Dijon-style mustard

Be as free and easy with the relish as you like. Use your imagination to mix colors and varieties of fruits and vegetables.

For Marinade: In a mixing bowl combine all marinade ingredients. Reserve ¼ *cup* of the marinade for the relish; cover and chill.

To Prepare Meat: Trim fat from meat. Place steak in a plastic bag set into a shallow dish. Pour remaining marinade over steak in bag. Seal bag and turn steak to coat well. Marinate in the refrigerator for 6 to 24 hours, turning bag occasionally.

For Relish: In a bowl combine reserved ¼ cup marinade and all relish ingredients. Cover and chill till serving time, up to 24 hours.

For Sauce: In a small mixing bowl stir together all sauce ingredients. Cover and chill till serving time, up to 24 hours.

To Cook by Indirect Grill Method: Remove the steak from bag, reserving marinade. In a covered grill arrange preheated coals around a drip pan. Test for *medium* heat above the pan. Place steak on the grill rack over the drip pan. Cover and grill to desired doneness (see chart), brushing occasionally with marinade the first half of cooking time.

To Cook by Direct Grill Method: Remove steak from bag, reserving marinade. Grill steak on the grill rack of an uncovered grill directly over *medium* coals for 6 minutes. Turn steak and brush with reserved marinade. Continue grilling to desired doneness (see chart).

Doneness	Indirect	Direct
Rare	22 to 26 minutes	14 to 18 minutes
Medium	26 to 30 minutes	18 to 22 minutes

To Serve: If desired, season steak with salt and pepper. Slice the meat into thin strips. Serve with relish and sauce.

Per serving: 335 calories / 28 g protein / 23 g carbohydrate / 14 g fat (5 g saturated) / 78 mg cholesterol / 109 mg sodium / 596 mg potassium.

Tequila-Lime Fajitas

| Indirect or Direct Grilling | Marinating Time: 6 to 24 hours | Serves 3 |

Marinade:	½ cup lime juice
	¼ cup tequila
	¼ cup cooking oil
	1 4-ounce can chopped green chili peppers, drained
	½ teaspoon bottled hot pepper sauce
	¼ teaspoon salt
Meat:	1 12-ounce boneless beef plate skirt steak *or* beef flank steak
	1 medium onion, thinly sliced
Tortillas:	6 8-inch flour *or* corn tortillas
Toppings:	⅔ cup salsa (optional)
	1 medium ripe avocado, pitted, peeled, and sliced (optional)
	½ cup dairy sour cream (optional)

It's Mexican night tonight! Blend some margaritas, fill a big bowl with chips, and serve these restaurant-style fajitas right off your very own grill.

For Marinade: In a medium mixing bowl combine all marinade ingredients.

To Prepare Meat: Place steak and onion in a plastic bag set into a shallow dish. Pour marinade over steak in bag. Seal bag and turn steak to coat well. Marinate in the refrigerator for 6 to 24 hours, turning bag occasionally. Remove steak from bag, reserving marinade.

Tear off a 36x18-inch piece of heavy foil. Fold in half to make a double thickness of foil that measures 18x18 inches. Using a slotted spoon, remove onion and green chili peppers from marinade and place them in the center of the foil. Bring up two opposite edges of foil and seal with a double fold. Then fold remaining ends to completely enclose the onions and peppers, leaving space for steam to build.

For Tortillas: Stack the tortillas and wrap in a double thickness of heavy foil.

To Cook by Indirect Grill Method: In a covered grill arrange preheated coals around a drip pan. Test for *medium* heat above the pan. Place steak and the wrapped onion and chili peppers on the grill rack over the drip pan. Cover and grill for 10 minutes. Brush steak with reserved marinade. Add wrapped tortillas to the grill rack. Continue grilling for 8 to 12 minutes more or till beef is desired doneness.

To Cook by Direct Grill Method: Grill steak and the wrapped onion and chili peppers on the grill rack of an uncovered grill directly over *medium* coals for 6 minutes. Turn steak and brush with reserved marinade. Add wrapped tortillas to the grill rack. Continue grilling for 6 to 8 minutes more or till beef is desired doneness.

To Serve: Thinly slice steak into bite-size pieces. Divide steak, onion, and chili peppers among the tortillas. Roll up tortillas. If desired, top with salsa and serve with avocado slices and sour cream.

Per serving: 481 calories / 26 g protein / 40 g carbohydrate / 21 g fat (4 g saturated) / 61 mg cholesterol / 280 mg sodium / 281 mg potassium.

Tequila-Lime Fajitas

Lemon-Dill Marinated Flank Steak

	Indirect or Direct Grilling	Marinating Time: 6 to 24 hours	Serves 4
Marinade:	2 green onions, sliced (¼ cup)		
	¼ cup water		
	¼ cup dry red wine		
	¼ cup soy sauce		
	3 tablespoons lemon juice		
	2 tablespoons cooking oil		
	1 tablespoon snipped fresh dill *or* 1 teaspoon dried dillweed		
	1 tablespoon Worcestershire sauce		
	2 cloves garlic, minced		
	½ teaspoon celery seed		
	½ teaspoon pepper		
Meat:	1 1- to 1½-pound beef flank steak, cut about ¾ inch thick		

A summer-style recipe—a marinade that's easy to put together, and a meat that's quick to grill.

For Marinade: In a medium mixing bowl combine all marinade ingredients.

To Prepare Meat: Score meat by making shallow cuts at 1-inch intervals diagonally across the steak in a diamond pattern. Repeat scoring on the second side. Place steak in a plastic bag set into a shallow dish. Pour marinade over steak in bag. Seal bag and turn steak to coat well. Marinate in the refrigerator for 6 to 24 hours, turning bag occasionally. Remove steak from bag, reserving marinade.

To Cook by Indirect Grill Method: In a covered grill arrange preheated coals around a drip pan. Test for *medium* heat above the pan. Place steak on the grill rack over the drip pan. Cover and grill for 18 to 22 minutes or till desired doneness, turning once and brushing with reserved marinade halfway through grilling time.

To Cook by Direct Grill Method: Grill steak on the grill rack of an uncovered grill directly over *medium* coals for 12 to 14 minutes or till desired doneness, turning once and brushing with reserved marinade halfway through grilling time.

To Serve: Slice the meat diagonally across the grain into very thin slices.

Per serving: 201 calories / 22 g protein / 1 g carbohydrate / 10 g fat (3 g saturated) / 53 mg cholesterol / 206 mg sodium / 357 mg potassium.

Marinated Blade Steaks

		Indirect Grilling	Marinating Time: 6 to 24 hours	Serves 4
Marinade:	1	4-ounce can chopped green chili peppers (undrained)		
	⅓	cup red wine vinegar		
	¼	cup olive oil *or* cooking oil		
	1	tablespoon hot-style mustard		
	2	teaspoons dried Italian seasoning, crushed		
	2	cloves garlic, minced		
Meat:	4	pork shoulder blade steaks, cut ½ inch thick (2 to 2½ pounds total)		
Sauce:	½	cup tomato sauce		
	1	tablespoon honey		

The savory marinade and sauce also taste great on beef flank steak.

For Marinade: In a small mixing bowl combine all marinade ingredients.

To Prepare Meat: Trim fat from meat. Place steaks in a plastic bag set into a shallow dish. Pour marinade over steaks in bag. Seal bag and turn steaks to coat well. Marinate in the refrigerator for 6 to 24 hours, turning bag occasionally. Remove steaks from bag, reserving ¼ *cup* of the marinade.

For Sauce: In a small saucepan combine sauce ingredients and ¼ cup reserved marinade. Bring to boiling; boil at least 1 minute. Remove from heat; set aside.

To Cook by Indirect Grill Method: In a covered grill arrange preheated coals around a drip pan. Test for *medium-high* heat above the pan. Place steaks on the grill rack over the drip pan. Cover and grill for 24 to 28 minutes or till pork is tender and no pink remains, brushing occasionally with sauce halfway through the grilling time. Pass remaining sauce with the meat.

Per serving: 544 calories / 41 g protein / 10 g carbohydrate / 38 g fat (10 g saturated) / 154 mg cholesterol / 489 mg sodium / 736 mg potassium.

Italian Sausage and Pepper Sandwiches

Indirect Grilling   Serves 4

Peppers:	2	medium green, red, *and/or* yellow sweet peppers, cut into julienne strips (2 cups)
	1	medium onion, chopped (½ cup)
	3	tablespoons Italian salad dressing
Meat:	4	fresh hot *or* mild Italian sausage links (¾ to 1 pound)
Bread:	4	French-style rolls, halved lengthwise

That's right, there's no cooking in your kitchen. You can prepare the pepper-onion mixture and the sausages on the grill.

For Peppers: Tear off a 36x18-inch piece of heavy foil. Fold in half to make a double thickness of foil that measures 18x18 inches. Toss together peppers and onion. Place pepper mixture in the center of the foil. Drizzle with salad dressing. Bring up two opposite edges of foil and seal with a double fold. Then fold remaining ends to completely enclose the peppers and onions, leaving space for steam to build. Refrigerate the packet till ready to grill.

To Cook by Indirect Grill Method: In a covered grill arrange preheated coals around a drip pan. Test for *medium* heat above the pan. Place the sausage links and the packet of the pepper mixture on the grill rack over the drip pan. Cover and grill for 20 to 25 minutes or till sausage juices run clear and peppers are very tender, turning sausage once.

To Serve: Split the rolls and toast on the grill. Serve sausages in the rolls and top each with some of the peppers and onion.

Per serving: 587 calories / 24 g protein / 64 g carbohydrate / 26 g fat (7 g saturated) / 49 mg cholesterol / 1,287 mg sodium / 385 mg potassium.

Bratwurst with Onions

Indirect Grilling   Marinating Time: 6 to 24 hours   Serves 8

Marinade:	1 12-ounce can beer
	2 tablespoons brown sugar
	1 tablespoon prepared mustard
	1 teaspoon chili powder
	Several dashes bottled hot pepper sauce
Meat:	8 fresh bratwurst (1½ to 2 pounds)
Onions:	3 medium onions, sliced
	3 tablespoons margarine or butter
	1 teaspoon chili powder
Bread:	8 French-style rolls, halved lengthwise

Some like it hot! For brats and onions with even more spiciness, use the chili powder labeled "hot".

For Marinade: In a small mixing bowl combine all marinade ingredients.

To Prepare Meat: Place bratwurst in a plastic bag set into a deep bowl. Pour marinade over bratwurst in bag. Seal bag and turn bratwurst to coat well. Marinate in the refrigerator for 6 to 24 hours, turning bag occasionally. Remove bratwurst from bag, reserving marinade.

For Onions: Tear off a 36x18-inch piece of heavy foil. Fold in half to make a double thickness of foil that measures 18x18 inches. Place onions in the center of the foil. Dot with margarine or butter; sprinkle with chili powder. Bring up two opposite edges of foil and seal with a double fold. Then fold remaining ends to completely enclose the onions, leaving space for steam to build. Refrigerate the packet till ready to grill.

To Cook by Indirect Grill Method: In a covered grill arrange preheated coals around a drip pan. Test for *medium* heat above the pan. Place the bratwurst on the grill rack over the drip pan. Cover and grill for 10 minutes. Place the packet of onions on the grill rack over the coals. Turn bratwurst and brush with reserved marinade. Cook for 10 to 15 minutes more or till sausage juices run clear and onions are tender.

To serve: Place bratwurst in rolls. Top each bratwurst with some of the onions.

Per serving: 630 calories / 23 g protein / 63 g carbohydrate / 31 g fat (9 g saturated) / 51 mg cholesterol / 1,158 mg sodium / 338 mg potassium.

Cheese-Stuffed Knockwurst

Indirect Grilling   Serves 5

Meat:	5 fully cooked knockwurst *or* fully cooked bratwurst (about 1 pound)
	2 ounces Monterey Jack cheese with caraway
	2 green onions, thinly sliced (¼ cup)
	5 slices bacon
Bread:	5 French-style rolls *or* frankfurter buns, halved lengthwise
	Catsup, mustard, *and/or* pickle relish (optional)

Stuff the knockwurst with cheese and wind the bacon around 'em. Then pack them up to grill at your favorite park for a picnic.

To Prepare Meat: Cut a lengthwise slit in each knockwurst or bratwurst about ½ inch deep. Cut cheese into 5 strips that are 2½x½x¼-inches. Insert a cheese strip and some of the green onion into each knockwurst. Wrap a slice of bacon around each knockwurst. Fasten the bacon with wooden toothpicks.

To Cook by Indirect Grill Method: In a covered grill arrange preheated coals around a drip pan. Test for *medium* heat above the pan. Place knockwurst, cheese side up, on the grill rack over the drip pan. Cover and grill for 8 to 10 minutes or till bacon is crisp and cheese is melted.

To Serve: Place knockwurst in French-style rolls or buns. If desired, serve with catsup, mustard, and/or pickle relish.

Per serving: 686 calories / 26 g protein / 65 g carbohydrate / 35 g fat (13 g saturated) / 68 mg cholesterol / 1,718 mg sodium / 329 mg potassium.

Cheese-Stuffed Knockwurst

Polish Sausage with Potatoes

Direct Grilling   Serves 4

Glaze:	¼ cup honey
	2 tablespoons brown mustard
	1 tablespoon vinegar
Potatoes	1½ pounds red potatoes
	2 tablespoons cooking oil
Meat:	1¼ pounds fully cooked Polish sausage ring or links

Here's a traditional country-style meal adapted for the grill.

For Glaze: In a small mixing bowl combine all glaze ingredients. Set aside.

For Potatoes: Cut the potatoes diagonally into 1-inch-thick slices. Brush both sides of each potato slice with oil.

To Cook by Direct Grill Method: Grill potato slices on the grill rack of an uncovered grill directly over *medium* coals about 15 minutes or till golden brown on one side. Turn potato slices. Grill about 10 minutes more or till nearly tender. Add sausage to the grill rack. Cover grill and cook for 5 to 8 minutes more or till potatoes are tender and sausage is heated through, turning once and brushing meat and potatoes occasionally with the glaze.

To Serve: Arrange potato slices on a large platter. Cut sausage into serving-size pieces. Place sausage on top of potatoes. Spoon sauce over potato and sausage slices.

Per serving: 508 calories / 16 g protein / 40 g carbohydrate / 32 g fat (10 g saturated) / 66 mg cholesterol / 905 mg sodium / 702 mg potassium.

Ham with Oranges

Indirect Grilling   Serves 6

Fruit:	2 medium oranges
	1 teaspoon snipped fresh mint *or* ¼ teaspoon dried mint, crushed
Glaze:	⅓ cup orange marmalade
	1 tablespoon lemon juice
	1 teaspoon prepared mustard
Meat:	1 1½-pound fully cooked center-cut ham slice, cut 1 inch thick

Dress up a simple cut of ham with a savory citrus glaze and minted oranges.

For Fruit: Peel and section oranges over a bowl to catch juice. In a medium mixing bowl toss together the juice, the orange sections, and the mint. Cover and chill till serving time.

For Glaze: In a small saucepan combine all glaze ingredients. Cook and stir over low heat till marmalade is melted.

To Cook by Indirect Grill Method: In a covered grill arrange preheated coals around a drip pan. Test for *medium-high* heat above the pan. Place ham steak on the grill rack over the drip pan. Cover and grill for 20 to 24 minutes or till heated through, turning once and brushing occasionally with glaze.

To Serve: Cut the ham steak into serving-size pieces. Spoon the orange mixture over the ham steak pieces.

Per serving: 249 calories / 24 g protein / 23 g carbohydrate / 6 g fat (2 g saturated) / 60 mg cholesterol / 1,378 mg sodium / 391 mg potassium.

Maple-and-Mustard-Glazed Ham Steak

Indirect Grilling   Serves 6

Glaze:	2	tablespoons margarine *or* butter
	¼	cup maple *or* maple-flavored syrup
	2	tablespoons brown mustard
Meat:	1	1½- to 2-pound fully cooked center-cut ham slice, cut 1 inch thick

Looking for a new recipe to serve for brunch? Take part of the cooking outdoors and grill up this sweet, yet tangy ham recipe.

For Glaze: In a small saucepan melt margarine or butter. Remove from heat. Stir in remaining glaze ingredients, stirring with whisk till smooth. Return to heat; bring to boiling. Reduce heat and cook for 1 to 2 minutes more to thicken slightly.

To Cook by Indirect Grill Method: In a covered grill arrange preheated coals around a drip pan. Test for *medium-high* heat above the pan. Place ham steak on the grill rack over the drip pan. Cover and grill for 20 to 24 minutes or till heated through, turning once and brushing occasionally with glaze.

Per serving: 228 calories / 24 g protein / 9 g carbohydrate / 10 g fat (2 g saturated) / 60 mg cholesterol / 1,428 mg sodium / 334 mg potassium.

From The Waters

If cooking fish and seafood is not your forte, give grilling a try. It's one of the easiest ways to net succulent results. Tackle these: Apple-Stuffed Trout, Tropical Halibut Steaks, Salmon with Toasted Pecans, or Scallops and Sweet Peppers. Superb!

Fish Steaks with Fresh Fruit Salsa

Indirect or Direct Grilling   Serves 4

Fruit Salsa:	1	small ripe nectarine
	½	small ripe papaya
	1	fresh jalapeño chili pepper* *or* 1 tablespoon capers, drained
	2	to 3 teaspoons snipped fresh rosemary *or* 1 teaspoon dried rosemary, crushed, *or* 2 to 3 teaspoons snipped fresh basil *or* ½ teaspoon dried basil, crushed
	1	tablespoon olive oil
Fish:	4	8-ounce fresh *or* frozen halibut, swordfish, shark, *or* salmon steaks, cut 1 inch thick (thawed, if frozen)
	2	tablespoons olive oil

Choose the fish steaks and salsa seasonings that suit your own taste. Then, brighten each serving with a fresh rosemary or basil sprig, a purple kale leaf, and steamed baby summer squash.

For Fruit Salsa: Remove the pit from the nectarine and chop fruit. Peel, seed, and chop the papaya. If using, seed and chop the jalapeño pepper. In a medium mixing bowl combine all fruit salsa ingredients. Cover and chill thoroughly. Set aside.

To Prepare Fish: Brush both sides of fish steaks with olive oil.

To Cook by Indirect Grill Method: In a covered grill arrange preheated coals around a drip pan. Test for *medium* heat above the pan. Place fish on the greased grill rack over the drip pan. Cover and grill for 8 to 12 minutes or just till fish begins to flake easily, turning once and brushing with olive oil halfway through grilling time.

To Cook by Direct Grill Method: Grill fish on the greased rack of an uncovered grill directly over *medium* coals for 8 to 12 minutes or just till fish begins to flake easily, turning once and brushing with olive oil halfway through grilling time.

To Serve: Serve fish with fruit salsa.

*Note: When seeding and chopping a fresh chili pepper, protect your hands with plastic gloves. The oils in the pepper can irritate your skin. Also, avoid direct contact with your eyes. When finished with the chili pepper, wash your hands thoroughly.

Per serving: 365 calories / 48 g protein / 7 g carbohydrate / 16 g fat (2 g saturated) / 73 mg cholesterol,124 mg sodium / 1 /173 mg potassium.

Fish Steaks with Fresh Fruit Salsa

Tuna Steaks with Hot Chili Pepper Sauce

Indirect or Direct Grilling   Serves 4

Sauce:	
	⅓ cup mayonnaise *or* salad dressing
	1 jalapeño pepper, finely chopped*
	1 tablespoon Dijon-style mustard
	1 teaspoon lemon juice
Fish:	Dash ground red pepper
	1 tablespoon olive oil *or* cooking oil
	4 6-ounce fresh *or* frozen tuna *or* halibut steaks, cut 1 inch thick (thawed, if frozen)

Prefer a hotter sauce to eat with the fish? Then be sure to include the jalapeño pepper seeds when finely chopping the pepper.

For Sauce: In a small mixing bowl combine all sauce ingredients. Cover and chill till serving time.

To Prepare Fish: Stir ground red pepper into oil. Brush both sides of tuna or halibut steaks with olive oil or cooking oil mixture.

To Cook by Indirect Grill Method: In a covered grill arrange preheated coals around a drip pan. Test for *medium* heat above the pan. Place fish on the greased grill rack over the drip pan. Cover and grill for 8 to 12 minutes or just till fish begins to flake easily, turning once and brushing with olive oil or cooking oil mixture halfway through grilling time.

To Cook by Direct Grill Method: Grill fish on the greased rack of an uncovered grill directly over *medium* coals for 8 to 12 minutes or just till fish begins to flake easily, turning once and brushing with olive oil or cooking oil mixture halfway through grilling time.

To Serve: Serve grilled fish with sauce.

*****Note:** When seeding and chopping a fresh chili pepper, protect your hands with plastic gloves. The oils in the pepper can irritate your skin. Also, avoid direct contact with your eyes. When finished with the chili pepper, wash your hands thoroughly.

Per serving: 462 calories / 44 g protein / 1 g carbohydrate / 31 g fat (5 g saturated) / 81 mg cholesterol / 333 mg sodium / 487 mg potassium.

Swordfish á la Thyme

Indirect or Direct Grilling	Marinating Time: 1 hour	Serves 4

Marinade:	¼ cup olive oil *or* cooking oil
	¼ cup white wine vinegar
	2 green onions, thinly sliced (¼ cup)
	1 teaspoon dried thyme, crushed
Fish:	4 6-ounce fresh *or* frozen swordfish *or* halibut steaks, cut 1 inch thick (thawed, if frozen)
Garnish:	Lemon wedges

Start your dinner preparations by marinating the fish. While the fish is in the refrigerator picking up the marinade's flavor, start fixing the rest of the meal. Possible accompaniments include a green vegetable, a sauced pasta, and sliced French bread toasted on the grill.

For Marinade: In a small mixing bowl combine all marinade ingredients.

To Prepare Fish: Place fish in a plastic bag set into a deep bowl. Pour marinade over fish in bag. Seal bag and turn fish to coat well. Marinate in the refrigerator for 1 hour, turning bag occasionally. Remove fish from bag, reserving marinade.

To Cook by Indirect Grill Method: In a covered grill arrange preheated coals around a drip pan. Test for *medium* heat above the pan. Place fish on the greased grill rack over the drip pan. Cover and grill for 8 to 12 minutes or just till fish begins to flake easily, turning once and brushing with reserved marinade halfway through grilling time.

To Cook by Direct Grill Method: Grill fish on the greased rack of an uncovered grill directly over *medium* coals for 8 to 12 minutes or just till fish begins to flake easily, turning once and brushing with reserved marinade halfway through grilling time.

To Serve: Garnish with lemon wedges.

Per serving: 329 calories / 34 g protein / 2 g carbohydrate / 20 g fat (4 g saturated) / 67 mg cholesterol / 153 mg sodium / 523 mg potassium.

Salmon with Toasted Pecans

Indirect or Direct Grilling   Serves 4

Sauce:	¼ cup dairy sour cream
	¼ cup mayonnaise *or* salad dressing
	1 teaspoon snipped fresh thyme *or* ¼ teaspoon dried thyme, crushed
	1 teaspoon lemon juice
	½ teaspoon prepared mustard
Fish:	4 6-ounce fresh *or* frozen salmon *or* halibut steaks, cut 1 inch thick (thawed, if frozen)
	2 tablespoons margarine *or* butter, melted
Garnish:	Romaine leaves (optional)
	¼ cup chopped toasted pecans
	Fresh thyme sprigs (optional)

To toast the pecans, spread the nuts in a single layer in a shallow baking pan. Bake in a 350° oven for 5 to 10 minutes or till light golden brown, stirring them once or twice.

For Sauce: In a small saucepan combine sauce ingredients. Cook and stir over low heat till hot. Cover and keep warm.

To Cook by Indirect Grill Method: In a covered grill arrange preheated coals around a drip pan. Test for *medium* heat above the pan. Place fish on the greased grill rack over the drip pan. Cover and grill for 8 to 12 minutes or just till fish begins to flake easily, turning once and brushing occasionally with the melted margarine or butter halfway through grilling time.

To Cook by Direct Grill Method: Grill fish on the greased rack of an uncovered grill directly over *medium* coals for 8 to 12 minutes or just till fish begins to flake easily, turning once and brushing occasionally with the melted margarine or butter halfway through grilling time.

To Serve: If desired, serve salmon steaks on romaine leaves. Serve sauce over salmon steaks. Sprinkle with pecans and, if desired, garnish with sprigs of fresh thyme.

Per serving: 382 calories / 26 g protein / 2 g carbohydrate / 30 g fat (6 g saturated) / 45 mg cholesterol / 1,201 mg sodium / 289 mg potassium.

Salmon with Toasted Pecans

Tropical Halibut Steaks

Indirect or Direct Grilling | Marinating Time: 1 hour | Serves 4

Marinade:	⅓ cup pineapple-orange juice
	⅓ cup soy sauce
	¼ teaspoon curry powder
Fish:	4 6-ounce fresh *or* frozen halibut steaks, cut 1 inch thick (thawed, if frozen)
Fruit Sauce:	1 8-ounce can pineapple chunks
	¼ of a medium cantaloupe *or* ½ of a papaya (1 cup)
	Dash curry powder
	2 teaspoons cornstarch
Garnish:	2 tablespoons toasted coconut

A sprinkling of toasted coconut accents the subtle curry and fruit flavors of the marinade and sauce. If you like, make extra toasted coconut and keep it on hand in the refrigerator to use as a quick garnish for other dishes.

For Marinade: In a small mixing bowl combine all marinade ingredients.

To Prepare Fish: Place fish in a plastic bag set into a deep bowl. Pour marinade over fish in bag. Seal bag and turn fish to coat well. Marinate in the refrigerator for 1 hour, turning bag occasionally. Remove fish from bag, reserving marinade.

To Prepare Fruit Sauce: Drain pineapple chunks, reserving juice. Peel and seed cantaloupe or papaya. Finely chop fruit. In a small saucepan combine chopped pineapple and cantaloupe or papaya and the curry powder. Add enough water to reserved pineapple juice to make ½ cup. Stir in cornstarch. Add pineapple juice mixture to fruit mixture in saucepan. Cook and stir over medium heat till thickened and bubbly. Cook and stir for 2 minutes more. Keep warm.

To Cook by Indirect Grill Method: In a covered grill arrange preheated coals around a drip pan. Test for *medium* heat above the pan. Place fish on the greased grill rack over the drip pan. Cover and grill for 8 to 12 minutes or just till fish begins to flake easily, turning once and brushing with reserved marinade halfway through grilling time.

To Cook by Direct Grill Method: Grill fish on the greased rack of an uncovered grill directly over *medium* coals for 8 to 12 minutes or just till fish begins to flake easily, turning once and brushing with reserved marinade halfway through grilling time.

To Serve: Spoon fruit sauce over grilled halibut. To garnish, sprinkle with toasted coconut.

Per serving: 256 calories / 36 g protein / 15 g carbohydrate / 5 g fat (1 g saturated) / 55 mg cholesterol / 351 mg sodium / 979 mg potassium.

Halibut Steaks with Green Onion Sauce

Indirect or Direct Grilling   Serves 4

Sauce:	6 green onions, sliced (¾ cup)
	1 clove garlic, minced
	2 tablespoons margarine *or* butter
	2 teaspoons all-purpose flour
	½ teaspoon dried chervil, crushed
	½ teaspoon instant chicken bouillon granules
	⅛ teaspoon salt
	¾ cup milk
Fish:	4 6-ounce fresh *or* frozen halibut *or* tuna steaks, cut 1 inch thick (thawed, if frozen)
	2 tablespoons olive oil *or* cooking oil

Chervil lends it's sweet licoricelike flavor to the savory green onion sauce.

For Sauce: In a small saucepan cook green onions and garlic in margarine or butter till onion is tender but not brown. Stir in flour, chervil, chicken bouillon granules, and salt. Add milk all at once. Cook and stir over medium heat till thickened and bubbly. Cook and stir for 1 minute more. Keep sauce warm while grilling fish.

To Prepare Fish: Brush both sides of halibut or tuna steaks with olive oil or cooking oil.

To Cook by Indirect Grill Method: In a covered grill arrange preheated coals around a drip pan. Test for *medium* heat above the pan. Place fish on the greased grill rack over the drip pan. Cover and grill for 8 to 12 minutes or just till fish begins to flake easily, turning once and brushing with olive oil or cooking oil halfway through grilling time.

To Cook by Direct Grill Method: Grill fish on the greased rack of an uncovered grill directly over *medium* coals for 8 to 12 minutes or just till fish begins to flake easily, turning once and brushing with olive oil or cooking oil halfway through grilling time.

To Serve: Serve sauce over grilled fish steaks.

Per serving: 327 calories / 37 g protein / 4 g carbohydrate / 17 g fat (3 g saturated) / 58 mg cholesterol / 357 mg sodium / 867 mg potassium.

Gingered Fish Fillets

Indirect or Direct Grilling	Marinating Time: 1 hour	Serves 4

Marinade:	2	tablespoons olive oil *or* cooking oil
	2	tablespoons rice vinegar *or* vinegar
	2	green onions, sliced (¼ cup)
	1½	teaspoons grated gingerroot
	1	teaspoon toasted sesame oil
Fish:	4	4-ounce fresh *or* frozen red snapper *or* whitefish fillets, cut ½ to ¾ inch thick (thawed, if frozen)
Vegetables:	1	medium tomato
	1	small green sweet pepper

Tomato wedges and green pepper rings add color to the tasty fish fillets.

For Marinade: In a small mixing bowl combine all marinade ingredients.

To Prepare Fish: Place fish in a plastic bag set into a deep bowl. Pour marinade over fish in bag. Seal bag and turn fish to coat well. Marinate in the refrigerator for 1 hour, turning bag occasionally. Remove fish from bag, reserving marinade. Cut several slits in an 18x18-inch piece of heavy foil. Grease foil and place fish on it.

To Prepare Vegetables: Cut the tomato into wedges and the green sweet pepper into rings. Place tomato wedges on 2 long metal skewers, leaving ¼ inch between pieces. Place sweet peppers on the foil.

To Cook by Indirect Grill Method: In a covered grill arrange preheated coals around a drip pan. Test for *medium* heat above the pan.

Place fish and peppers on the grill rack over the drip pan. Cover and grill for 10 to 11 minutes or just till fish begins to flake easily, brushing with reserved marinade after 6 minutes. Add tomato wedges to foil the last 3 minutes of grilling.

To Cook by Direct Grill Method: Grill fish and sweet peppers on the rack of an uncovered grill directly over *medium* coals for 4 minutes. Turn fish and brush with reserved marinade. Add tomato wedges. Cook for 2 to 4 minutes more or just till fish begins to flake easily and the sweet pepper is crisp-tender.

Per serving: 194 calories / 24 g protein / 3 g carbohydrate / 10 g fat (1 g saturated) / 42 mg cholesterol / 53 mg sodium / 572 mg potassium.

Speedy Salmon Fillet

Indirect or Direct Grilling   Serves 6

Sauce:	3	tablespoons lemon juice
	1	tablespoon cooking oil
	1	tablespoon soy sauce
	1	teaspoon grated gingerroot *or* ¼ teaspoon ground ginger
	1	teaspoon Worcestershire sauce
	1	clove garlic, minced
	¼	teaspoon pepper
Fish:	1	1½-pound boneless, skinless fresh *or* frozen salmon fillet (thawed, if frozen)

Use either fresh gingerroot or ground ginger to flavor the sauce. If you choose to use fresh ginger, grate what you need and freeze the rest of the root in a moisture- and vaporproof bag until it's needed for other recipes.

For Sauce: In a small mixing bowl combine all sauce ingredients. Set aside.

To Prepare Fish: Brush both sides of salmon with some sauce. For indirect grill cooking, cut several slits in a piece of heavy foil large enough to hold fish. Grease foil and place fish on it. Or, for direct grill cooking, place salmon in a greased grill basket or on greased foil as above; turn under the thin ends of the fillet to make an even thickness. Measure thickness of fillet. Close basket.

To Cook by Indirect Grill Method: In a covered grill arrange preheated coals around a drip pan. Test for *medium* heat above the pan. Place foil with fish on the grill rack over the drip pan. Cover and grill salmon for 14 to 16 minutes or just till fish begins to flake easily, brushing twice with sauce.

To Cook by Direct Grill Method: Grill fish in basket or on foil on an uncovered grill directly over *medium* coals for 4 to 6 minutes per ½ inch thickness of fish or just till fish begins to flake easily, turning once and brushing often with sauce.

Grilling Fish

Because fish is delicate and breaks apart easily, it helps to place the fish on foil or in a grill basket when grilling. Use a grill basket for direct grilling only; most grill basket handles can't take the heat of indirect cooking on a covered grill. To keep the fish from sticking, lightly grease or brush the foil or basket with cooking oil before adding the fish.

To avoid poaching fish in its own juices during grilling, cut slits in the foil and allow the juices to run through. Place a drip pan underneath to catch the juices.

If necessary to turn the fish during cooking, use a wide spatula and gently slide it under the fish.

Firmer-textured fish steaks can be grilled on a greased grill rack.

Per serving: 129 calories / 16 g protein / 1 g carbohydrate / 6 g fat (1 g saturated) / 20 mg cholesterol / 873 mg sodium / 181 mg potassium.

Fish and Shrimp Roulades

Fish and Shrimp Roulades

Indirect Grilling   Serves 4

Fish:		
	1	tablespoon lemon juice
	4	3- to 4-ounce fresh *or* frozen sole fillets, cut ¼ to ½ inch thick (thawed, if frozen)
Filling:	2	green onions, thinly sliced (¼ cup)
	2	teaspoons margarine *or* butter
	½	cup snipped parsley
	1	tablespoon snipped fresh basil *or* 1 teaspoon dried basil, crushed
	½	cup coarsely chopped cooked shrimp
	2	tablespoons fine dry bread crumbs
	¼	teaspoon instant chicken bouillon granules
Roulades:	1	tablespoon margarine *or* butter, melted
Sauce:	¼	cup coarsely chopped, cooked shrimp
	3	tablespoons margarine *or* butter
	1	tablespoon lemon juice
	1	teaspoon snipped fresh basil *or* ¼ teaspoon dried basil, crushed
Garnish:		Lemon wedges (optional)

You may have to piece together smaller fillet portions to make the 3- to 4-ounce fillets needed to roll around the filling. Secure the rolls with wooden toothpicks, but remember to remove the picks before serving. Round out the menu with a lightly cooked, fresh vegetable assortment and a fresh fruit salad.

To Prepare Fish: Drizzle lemon juice over fish fillets. Cover and chill in the refrigerator while preparing filling.

For Filling: In a small saucepan cook sliced green onion in margarine or butter for

1 minute. Add parsley and basil. Cook and stir for 1 minute more. Remove from heat. Stir in shrimp, bread crumbs, and the chicken bouillon granules.

To Prepare Roulades: Place *one-fourth* (about 3 tablespoons) of the filling at *one* end of *each* fillet. Roll fish up jelly-roll style. Secure each roulade with wooden toothpicks. Tear off a 24x18-inch piece of heavy foil. Fold to make a piece that measures 12x18 inches. Cut several slits in the foil. Place fish on foil. Brush each roulade with some of the melted margarine or butter.

For Sauce: In a small saucepan combine all sauce ingredients. Cook and stir till heated through. Keep sauce warm while grilling fish.

To Cook by Indirect Grill Method: In a covered grill arrange preheated coals around a drip pan. Test for *medium* heat above the pan. Place foil with roulades on the grill rack over the drip pan. Cover and grill for 14 to 16 minutes or just till fish begins to flake easily.

To Serve: Remove toothpicks. Spoon sauce over fish. Garnish fish with lemon wedges, if desired.

Per serving: 252 calories / 19 g protein / 2 g carbohydrate / 18 g fat (4 g saturated) / 81 mg cholesterol / 374 mg sodium / 315 mg potassium.

Salmon Fillet with Orange-Basil Sauce

Indirect or Direct Grilling   Serves 6

Sauce:	¼ cup frozen orange juice concentrate, thawed
	3 tablespoons olive oil *or* cooking oil
	2 tablespoons snipped fresh basil *or* 1 teaspoon dried basil, crushed
	2 tablespoons water
	1 tablespoon snipped fresh mint *or* tarragon *or* ½ teaspoon dried mint *or* tarragon, crushed
	1 tablespoon Worcestershire sauce
	2 cloves garlic, minced
Fish:	1 1½-pound boneless, skinless fresh *or* frozen salmon fillet (thawed, if frozen)
Vegetables:	4 small zucchini *and/or* yellow summer squash

The squash accompaniment cooks on its own piece of foil, right next to the fish. Because the squash cooks faster than the fish, add the squash to the grill after the fish is partly cooked.

For Sauce: In a small mixing bowl combine all sauce ingredients.

To Prepare Fish: Brush both sides of salmon with some sauce. For indirect grill cooking, cut several slits in a piece of heavy foil large enough to hold fish. Grease foil and place fish on it. Or, for direct grill cooking, place salmon in a greased grill basket or on greased foil as above; turn under the thin ends of the fillet to make an even thickness. Measure thickness of fillet. Close basket.

To Prepare Vegetables: Cut zucchini and/or squash in half lengthwise.

To Cook by Indirect Grill Method: In a covered grill arrange preheated coals around a drip pan. Test for *medium* heat above the pan. Place foil with fish on the grill rack over the drip pan. Cover and grill salmon for 14 to 16 minutes or just till fish begins to flake easily.

Place vegetables on a piece of heavy foil on grill rack next to fish. Grill vegetables directly over *medium-hot* coals the last 8 to 10 minutes of grilling or till vegetables are tender, turning the vegetables once and brushing fish and vegetables often with sauce.

To Cook by Direct Grill Method: Grill fish in basket or on foil on an uncovered grill directly over *medium* coals for 4 to 6 minutes per ½ inch thickness of fish or just till fish begins to flake easily. Place vegetables on a piece of heavy foil on grill rack next to fish. Grill vegetables the last 5 to 6 minutes of grilling or till vegetables are tender, turning fish and vegetables once and brushing often with sauce.

To Serve: If desired, garnish with fresh mint or basil. Serve with any remaining sauce.

Per serving: 196 calories / 17 g protein / 8 g carbohydrate / 11 g fat (2 g saturated) / 20 mg cholesterol / 719 mg sodium / 373 mg potassium.

Grilled Red Snapper with Crabmeat Stuffing

Indirect Grilling   Serves 6

Wood Chips:	3 to 4 cups mesquite wood chips (optional)
Stuffing:	1 cup sliced fresh mushrooms
	2 tablespoons margarine *or* butter
	1 pound lump crabmeat *or* two 7-ounce cans crabmeat
Sauce:	2 tablespoons olive oil *or* cooking oil
	1 tablespoon lime juice
	⅛ teaspoon garlic powder
Seasoning Rub:	1 tablespoon old Bay seasoning
	1 teaspoon sugar
	1 teaspoon pepper
	¾ teaspoon onion salt
	¾ teaspoon ground ginger
	¾ teaspoon ground cinnamon
	¾ teaspoon crushed red pepper
	¼ teaspoon salt
	⅛ teaspoon ground cloves
Fish:	1 3-pound *or* two 1½-pound fresh *or* frozen dressed red snapper (with head and tail) (thawed, if frozen)

Mesquite wood chips give the fish a smoky flavor. However, since the woods chips are optional, you'll still get plenty of flavor from the seasoning rub and the elegant stuffing.

To Prepare Wood Chips: If using, at least 1 hour before grilling, soak wood chips in enough water to cover. Drain the chips before using.

For Stuffing: In a large saucepan cook mushrooms in margarine or butter till tender. If using canned crabmeat, drain and flake it, removing any cartilage. Stir crabmeat into mushrooms; set aside.

For Sauce: In a small mixing bowl combine all sauce ingredients; set aside.

For Seasoning Rub: In a small mixing bowl combine all seasoning rub ingredients; set aside.

To Prepare Fish: Spoon stuffing into the fish cavity. Skewer the cavity closed with wooden toothpicks. Brush fish with sauce. Rub fish on both sides with seasoning rub. Cut several slits in a piece of heavy foil large enough to hold fish. Grease foil and place fish on it. Place any remaining stuffing in the center of a double thickness of heavy foil. Bring up two opposite edges of foil and seal with a double fold. Then fold remaining ends to completely enclose the stuffing, leaving space for steam to build. Refrigerate the packet till ready to grill.

To Cook by Indirect Grill Method: In a covered grill arrange preheated coals around a drip pan. Test for *medium* heat above the pan. If using, sprinkle drained wood chips onto the preheated coals. Place foil with fish on the grill rack over the drip pan. Cover and grill for 45 to 55 minutes for large fish and 35 to 45 minutes for smaller fish or just till fish begins to flake easily, drizzling occasionally with remaining sauce. Place packet of stuffing on the grill rack directly over *medium-hot* coals the last 15 minutes of grilling. Remove toothpicks before serving.

Per serving: 198 calories / 23 g protein / 3 g carbohydrate / 10 g fat (2 g saturated) / 53 mg cholesterol / 1,164 mg sodium / 421 mg potassium.

Grilled Trout with Fennel Stuffing

Grilled Tomatoes with Pesto
(see recipe, page 180)

Grilled Trout with Fennel Stuffing

Indirect Grilling | Serves 4

Stuffing:	2	heads fennel
	1	clove garlic, minced
	¼	teaspoon salt
	⅛	teaspoon pepper
	2	tablespoons margarine *or* butter
	1	tablespoon snipped parsley
Sauce:	3	tablespoons margarine *or* butter
	1	tablespoon lemon juice
	½	teaspoon dried rosemary, crushed
		Dash pepper
Fish:	4	8- to 10-ounce fresh *or* frozen dressed trout *or* other fish (thawed, if frozen)
Garnish:		Lemon wedges
		Parsley

Need a menu suggestion? Accompany the stuffed fish with Grilled Tomatoes with Pesto (see recipe, page 180) and a mixture of white and wild rice.

For Stuffing: Discard top and outer pieces of fennel. Chop fennel heads. (Should have about 2½ cups.) In a medium saucepan cook and stir fennel, garlic, salt, and pepper in margarine or butter for 10 minutes or till fennel is tender but not brown. Stir in parsley. Set aside.

For Sauce: In a small saucepan combine all sauce ingredients. Heat through.

To Prepare Fish: Spoon *one-fourth* of the stuffing into *each* fish cavity. Skewer the cavity closed with wooden toothpicks. Brush fish with sauce. Cut several slits in a piece of heavy foil large enough to hold fish. Grease foil and place fish on it.

To Cook by Indirect Grill Method: In a covered grill arrange preheated coals around a drip pan. Test for *medium* heat above the pan. Place foil with fish on the grill rack over the drip pan. Cover and grill for 15 to 20 minutes or just till fish begins to flake easily, brushing frequently with sauce.

To serve: Remove toothpicks. If desired, garnish with lemon and parsley.

Per serving: 409 calories / 47 g protein / 3 g carbohydrate / 22 g fat (4 g saturated) / 130 mg cholesterol / 376 mg sodium / 1,263 mg potassium.

Apple-Stuffed Trout

Indirect Grilling   Serves 4

Stuffing:	¼	cup snipped dried apple
	1½	cups corn bread stuffing mix
	2	tablespoons chopped hazelnuts (filberts) *or* pecans, toasted
	1	tablespoon thinly sliced green onion
	1	tablespoon margarine *or* butter, melted
	¼	cup water
	¼	teaspoon instant chicken bouillon granules
Fish:	4	8- to 10-ounce fresh *or* frozen dressed trout *or* other fish (thawed, if frozen)

If all the stuffing doesn't fit into the fish cavities, place any extra stuffing in a foil pouch. Heat on the grill the last few minutes of cooking.

For Stuffing: In a small mixing bowl combine snipped dried apple and enough *boiling water* to cover. Let stand 5 minutes. Drain. In a medium mixing bowl stir together the drained apple, stuffing mix, hazelnuts or pecans, green onion, and margarine or butter. In another small bowl stir together the ¼ cup water and the bouillon granules. Toss stuffing mixture with the water-bouillon mixture. Add an additional 1 tablespoon water if mixture is too dry.

To Prepare Fish: Spoon *one-fourth* of the stuffing into *each* fish cavity. Skewer the cavity closed with wooden toothpicks. Cut several slits in a piece of heavy foil large enough to hold fish. Grease foil and place fish on it.

To Cook By Indirect Grill Method: In a covered grill arrange preheated coals around a drip pan. Test for *medium* heat above the pan. Place foil with fish on the grill rack over the drip pan. Cover and grill for 20 to 25 minutes or just till fish begins to flake easily. Remove toothpicks before serving.

Per serving: 456 calories / 51 g protein / 29 g carbohydrate / 14 g fat (2 g saturated) / 130 mg cholesterol / 514 mg sodium / 1,172 mg potassium.

Grilled Crab Legs with Dipping Sauce

Indirect or Direct Grilling   Serves 4

Seafood:	12	fresh *or* frozen cooked crab legs (thawed, if frozen) (about 3 pounds)
	2	tablespoons margarine *or* butter
Sauce:	1	green onion, sliced (2 tablespoons)
	1	teaspoon dried dillweed
	1	tablespoon margarine *or* butter
	½	cup dairy sour cream
	¼	cup mayonnaise *or* salad dressing
	⅛	teaspoon ground red pepper

Go ahead and splurge! Serve crab legs with a dilled dipping sauce for a special treat. The king crab legs called for in this recipe come precooked and only need to be heated before serving.

To Prepare Seafood: Split whole crab legs in half lengthwise. To split them, use a kitchen shears to cut shell along top and bottom, then cut the meat in between. In a small saucepan melt the margarine or butter.

For Sauce: In a small saucepan cook green onion and dillweed in margarine or butter till onion is just tender. Stir in remaining sauce ingredients. Heat mixture through. *Do not boil.*

To Cook by Indirect Grill Method: In a covered grill arrange preheated coals around a drip pan. Test for *medium* heat above the pan. Place split crab legs, shell side down, on the grill rack over the drip pan. Cover and grill for 10 to 12 minutes or till heated through, brushing with the melted margarine or butter halfway through grilling time.

To Cook by Direct Grill Method: Place split crab legs, shell side down, on the grill rack of an uncovered grill directly over *medium* coals. Grill for 8 minutes or till heated through, brushing with the melted margarine or butter halfway through grilling time.

To Serve: Serve crab legs with sauce.

Per serving: 375 calories / 29 g protein / 2 g carbohydrate / 28 g fat (7 g saturated) / 96 mg cholesterol / 1,715 mg sodium / 435 mg potassium.

Raspberry Shrimp Salad

Indirect or Direct Grilling   Serves 4

Vinaigrette:	1 cup fresh raspberries
	¼ cup olive oil *or* salad oil
	¼ cup white wine vinegar *or* white vinegar
	1 teaspoon sugar
	½ teaspoon finely shredded orange peel
	¼ teaspoon dry mustard
Vegetables:	1 cup fresh pea pods
Seafood:	1 pound fresh *or* frozen jumbo shrimp in shells (16 per pound) (thawed, if frozen)
Greens:	6 cups torn red-tip leaf lettuce
Fruit:	1 cup raspberries

When the temperature soars, plan a luncheon or supper around this refreshing salad. Round out the meal with warm rolls or crusty French bread slices and a luscious chocolate dessert.

For Vinaigrette: In a blender container or food processor bowl combine all vinaigrette ingredients. Cover and blend or process till smooth. Set aside.

To Prepare Vegetable: Remove tips and strings from pea pods. In a small saucepan cook pea pods, covered, in a small amount of boiling water for 2 to 4 minutes or till crisp-tender. Drain. Set aside.

To Prepare Seafood: Peel and devein shrimp. To butterfly shrimp, make a deeper slit along its back; do not cut all the way through the shellfish. Lay the shrimp on a flat surface so that the sides open to resemble a butterfly. On 4 long metal skewers, loosely thread shrimp, leaving about ¼ inch between pieces.

To Cook by Indirect Grill Method: In a covered grill arrange preheated coals around a drip pan. Test for *medium* heat above the pan. Place skewers on the grill rack over the drip pan. Cover and grill for 8 to 10 minutes or till shrimp turn opaque.

To Cook by Direct Grill Method: Grill skewers on the grill rack of an uncovered grill directly over *medium* coals for 6 to 8 minutes or till shrimp turn opaque, turning once.

To Serve: Arrange torn lettuce and the pea pods on 4 dinner plates. Divide grilled shrimp among the plates. Top *each* plate with ¼ *cup* raspberries. Serve with vinaigrette.

Per serving: 246 calories / 17 g protein / 14 g carbohydrate / 15 g fat (2 g saturated) / 131 mg cholesterol / 158 mg sodium / 512 mg potassium.

Raspberry Shrimp Salad

Asparagus and Shrimp with Dill Butter

Indirect or Direct Grilling   Serves 4

Vegetables:	1 pound fresh asparagus
	1 medium leek
Butter:	¼ cup margarine *or* butter, softened
	1 tablespoon snipped fresh dill *or* 1 teaspoon dried dillweed
	1 tablespoon dry white wine
	½ teaspoon finely shredded lemon peel
	⅛ teaspoon salt
	⅛ teaspoon pepper
Seafood:	12 ounces fresh *or* frozen peeled and deveined shrimp (thawed, if frozen)
Accompaniment:	3 cups hot cooked rice *or* pasta

Cook the seafood and vegetables all in one packet for a main dish that's easy to cook and serve. You won't have any flare-ups on the grill, because the food is all neatly sealed in foil.

To Prepare Vegetables: Break off and discard woody bases from asparagus where spears snap easily. Cut asparagus into 2-inch pieces. Thinly slice leek.

For Butter: In a medium mixing bowl, stir together all butter ingredients.

To Prepare Packet: Tear off a 36x18-inch piece of heavy foil. Fold in half to make a double thickness of foil that measures 18x18 inches. Place shrimp and vegetables in the center of foil. Dollop with butter mixture. Bring up two opposite edges of foil and seal with a double fold. Then fold remaining ends to completely enclose the shrimp and vegetables, leaving space for steam to build.

To Cook by Indirect Grill Method: In a covered grill arrange preheated coals for indirect grilling. Test for *medium* heat where the packet will cook. Place foil packet on the grill rack not over the coals. Cover and grill for about 20 minutes or till shrimp turn opaque, turning once.

To Cook by Direct Grill Method: Grill foil packet on the grill rack of an uncovered grill directly over *medium* coals for about 15 minutes or till shrimp turn opaque, turning packet once.

To Serve: Serve shrimp-vegetable mixture on rice or pasta, spooning juices over.

Per serving: 395 calories / 20 g protein / 49 g carbohydrate / 13 g fat (3 g saturated) / 131 mg cholesterol / 360 mg sodium / 431 mg potassium.

Scallops and Sweet Peppers

Indirect or Direct Grilling	Marinating Time: 1 to 2 hours	Serves 4

Marinade:	2 tablespoons lemon juice
	2 tablespoons finely chopped shallot (about 1 shallot)
	1 tablespoon olive oil *or* salad oil
	1 tablespoon water
	⅛ teaspoon salt
	Dash pepper
Seafood:	1 pound fresh *or* frozen sea scallops (thawed, if frozen)
Vegetables:	1 medium red *and/or* yellow sweet pepper
	1 cup fresh pea pods

Use the larger sea scallops instead of the smaller bay or calico scallops when preparing this recipe.

For Marinade: In a small mixing bowl combine all marinade ingredients.

To Prepare Seafood: Cut any large scallops in half. Place scallops in a plastic bag set into a deep bowl. Pour marinade over scallops in bag. Seal bag and turn scallops to coat well. Marinate in the refrigerator for 1 to 2 hours, turning bag occasionally.

To Prepare Vegetables: Cut sweet pepper into 1-inch pieces. Remove tips and strings from pea pods. Cut pea pods in half crosswise. Add peppers and pea pods to marinated scallops; toss to mix.

To Prepare Mixture: Tear off a 36x18-inch piece of heavy foil. Fold in half to make a double thickness of foil that measures 18x18 inches. Place scallop and vegetable mixture with marinade in the center of the foil. Bring up two opposite edges of foil and seal with a double fold. Then fold remaining ends to completely enclose the scallops and vegetables, leaving space for steam to build.

To Cook by Indirect Grill Method: In a covered grill arrange preheated coals for indirect grilling. Test for *medium* heat where packet will cook. Place foil packet on the grill rack not over the coals. Cover and grill about 25 minutes or till scallops turn opaque, turning once.

To Cook by Direct Grill Method: Grill foil packet on the grill rack of an uncovered grill directly over *medium* coals about 25 minutes or till scallops turn opaque, turning once.

To Serve: Serve scallops and vegetables with a slotted spoon.

Per serving: 123 calories / 16 g protein / 6 g carbohydrate / 4 g fat (0 g saturated) / 34 mg cholesterol / 238 mg sodium / 423 mg potassium.

Brie-Stuffed Lobster Tails

Indirect or Direct Grilling   Serves 4

Stuffing:		
	2	tablespoons chopped onion
	1	tablespoon margarine *or* butter
	1	cup soft bread crumbs (about 1½ slices)
	1	ounce diced brie *or* shredded Monterey Jack cheese
	1	tablespoon snipped parsley
Seafood:	4	medium fresh *or* frozen rock lobster tails (about 5 ounces each) (thawed, if frozen)
	¼	cup margarine *or* butter, melted

Just when you thought lobster tails couldn't get any richer—we added a cheesy stuffing. If using the brie, dice the cheese, rind and all.

For Stuffing: In a small saucepan cook onion in margarine or butter till tender but not brown. Stir in bread crumbs, cheese, and parsley. Set aside.

To Prepare Seafood: Rinse lobster tails and pat dry with paper towels. Butterfly tails, by using kitchen shears or a sharp knife to cut lengthwise through centers of hard top shells and meat. Cut to, *but not through*, bottom shells. Using fingers, press shell halves of tails apart. Brush lobster meat with some of the melted margarine or butter.

To Cook by Indirect Grill Method: In a covered grill arrange preheated coals around a drip pan. Test for *medium* heat above the pan. Place lobster tails, meat side down, on the grill rack over the drip pan. Cover and grill for 10 minutes. Remove from grill. Brush lobster meat with more melted margarine or butter. Lightly pack *one-fourth* of stuffing into *each* lobster cavity. Continue indirect grilling, stuffing side up, for 6 to 8 minutes or till lobster meat turns opaque.

To Cook by Direct Grill Method: Grill lobster tails, meat side down, on the grill rack of an uncovered grill directly over *medium* coals for 6 minutes. Remove from grill. Brush lobster meat with more melted margarine or butter. Lightly pack *one-fourth* of stuffing into *each* lobster cavity. Continue direct grilling, stuffing side up, for 6 to 8 minutes or till meat turns opaque.

Per serving: 260 calories / 19 g protein / 7 g carbohydrate / 17 g fat (4 g saturated) / 63 mg cholesterol / 566 mg sodium / 318 mg potassium.

GRILLING ON SKEWERS

What do chicken, beef, shrimp, salmon, vegetables, and fruit have in common? They all thread up easily on skewers for super-simple barbecues! Need a quick appetizer, entrée, side dish or dessert? Get on the stick—you'll be minutes away from good eating!

Greek Kabobs with Walnut-Bulgur Pilaf

Indirect or Direct Grilling   Marinating Time: 2 to 6 hours   Serves 4

Marinade:	⅓ cup olive oil *or* cooking oil
	⅓ cup lemon juice
	⅓ cup water
	¾ teaspoon dried oregano, crushed
	½ teaspoon salt
	¼ teaspoon pepper
	1 clove garlic, minced
Meat:	1 pound lean boneless leg of lamb
	or beef sirloin
Vegetables:	1 small yellow summer squash
	4 small purple *or* white boiling onions
	1 cup broccoli flowerets
	½ cup fresh pea pods
	½ medium red *or* green sweet pepper
Pilaf:	Walnut-Bulgur Pilaf
	(see recipe, page 173)

Partially precooking selected vegetables before grilling them on skewers helps ensure that they'll be properly cooked when the meat is done. The pepper pieces on these kabobs stay crunchy because they're not precooked.

For Marinade: In a small mixing bowl combine all marinade ingredients.

To Prepare Meat: Trim fat from meat. Cut lamb or beef into 1-inch pieces. Place meat in a plastic bag set into a deep bowl. Pour marinade over meat in bag. Seal bag and turn meat to coat well. Marinate in the refrigerator for 2 to 6 hours, turning bag occasionally.

To Prepare Vegetables: Cut squash into ¼-inch-thick slices. Remove tips and strings from pea pods. In a small saucepan cook onions, covered, in a small amount of boiling water for 2 minutes. Add broccoli; continue cooking for 1 minute. Add squash and pea pods; continue cooking for 1 minute more.

Drain. Cut red or green sweet pepper into 1-inch pieces. Set all vegetables aside.

To Prepare Kabobs: Remove meat pieces from bag, reserving ¼ *cup* marinade. On 4 long metal skewers, alternately thread the meat and vegetables, leaving about ¼ inch between pieces.

To Cook by Indirect Grill Method: In a covered grill arrange preheated coals around a drip pan. Test for *medium* heat above the pan. Place kabobs on the grill rack over the drip pan. Cover and grill for 16 to 18 minutes or till meat is desired doneness, brushing with reserved marinade halfway through grilling time. Place the foil packet of pilaf beside the kabobs on the grill rack. Grill foil packet directly over *medium-high* coals the last 8 to 10 minutes of grilling or till heated through, turning packet frequently.

To Cook by Direct Grill Method: Grill kabobs on grill rack of uncovered grill directly over *medium* coals for 12 to 14 minutes or till meat is desired doneness, turning kabobs once and brushing with reserved marinade halfway through grilling time. Place the foil packet of pilaf beside the kabobs on grill rack. Grill foil packet directly over *medium* coals the last 8 to 10 minutes of grilling or till heated through; turn packet frequently.

To Serve: Serve the kabobs with Walnut-Bulgur Pilaf.

Per serving: 255 calories / 20 g protein / 9 g carbohydrate / 15 g fat (3 g saturated) / 57 mg cholesterol / 186 mg sodium / 496 mg potassium.

Greek Kabobs with Walnut-Bulgur Pilaf

Hidden Surprise Kabobs

Indirect or Direct Grilling   Serves 4

Meat Mixture:	1 beaten egg
	¼ cup fine dry bread crumbs
	1 tablespoon snipped parsley
	1 teaspoon dried Italian seasoning *or*
	basil, crushed
	1 pound ground beef
	¼ teaspoon salt
	⅛ teaspoon pepper
Sauce:	Honey-Mustard Brush-On Sauce
	(see recipe, page 201)
Vegetables:	12 small whole fresh mushrooms
	12 ½-inch cubes Swiss *or* Monterey Jack
	cheese (3 ounces)
	1 medium yellow *and/or* green
	sweet pepper
	1 medium onion
	4 to 6 cherry tomatoes

Guess what surprise is hidden inside these meatballs? It's a whole mushroom stuffed with a cheese cube. Besides adding flavor, the filled mushrooms help keep the meatballs on the skewers.

To Prepare Meat Mixture: In a large mixing mixing bowl combine all meat mixture ingredients *except* beef. Add beef; mix well. Set aside.

For Sauce: Prepare Honey-Mustard Brush-On Sauce. Set aside.

To Prepare Vegetables: Remove stems from mushrooms. Place *one* cube of cheese in *each* mushroom cap. Cut yellow and/or green sweet pepper into 1-inch pieces. Cut onion into 1-inch pieces. In a small saucepan cook onion, covered, in a small amount of boiling water for 2 minutes. Drain. Set all vegetables aside.

To Prepare Kabobs: Using a scant ¼ *cup* of the meat mixture, form a ball around *one* of the stuffed mushrooms, sealing well. Repeat with remaining meat mixture and mushrooms. On 4 long metal skewers, alternately thread meatballs, pepper pieces, and onion pieces, leaving about ¼ inch between each.

To Cook by Indirect Grill Method: In a covered grill arrange preheated coals around a drip pan. Test for *medium* heat above the pan. Place kabobs on the grill rack over the drip pan. Cover and grill about 25 minutes or till no pink remains and juices run clear, turning once. Add a cherry tomato to each skewer and brush generously with Honey-Mustard Brush-On Sauce the last 1 to 2 minutes of grilling.

To Cook by Direct Grill Method: Grill kabobs on the grill rack of an uncovered grill directly over *medium* coals about 25 minutes or till no pink remains and juices run clear, turning often. Add a cherry tomato to each skewer and brush generously with Honey-Mustard Brush-On Sauce the last 1 to 2 minutes of grilling.

Per serving: 463 calories / 32 g protein / 34 g carbohydrate / 22 g fat (10 g saturated) / 144 mg cholesterol / 554 mg sodium / 710 mg potassium.

Herb-Tomato Beef Kabobs

Indirect or Direct Grilling

Serves 4

Sauce:	⅔ cup tomato juice
	½ of a 0.7-ounce envelope (2½ teaspoons) Italian dry salad dressing mix
	1 teaspoon cornstarch
Meat:	1 pound boneless beef sirloin steak, cut 1 inch thick
Vegetables:	1 medium green or red sweet pepper
	8 whole fresh mushrooms
	4 cherry tomatoes

Cherry tomatoes take little time to heat. That's why they're added to the kabob skewers the last minute or two of grilling.

For Sauce: In a saucepan combine all sauce ingredients. Cook and stir till bubbly. Cook and stir for 2 minutes more. Set aside.

To Prepare Meat: Trim fat from meat. Cut meat into 1-inch pieces.

To Prepare Vegetables: Cut green or red sweet pepper into 1-inch pieces.

To Prepare Kabobs: On 4 long metal skewers, alternately thread beef, green or red sweet pepper, and mushrooms, leaving about ¼ inch between pieces.

To Cook by Indirect Grill Method: In a covered grill arrange preheated coals around a drip pan. Test for *medium* heat above the pan. Place kabobs on grill rack over the drip pan. Cover and grill for 16 to 18 minutes or till beef is desired doneness, brushing with sauce halfway through grilling time. Add a cherry tomato to each skewer the last 1 to 2 minutes of grilling. Brush with sauce before serving.

To Cook by Direct Grill Method: Grill kabobs on the grill rack of an uncovered grill directly over *medium* coals for 12 to 14 minutes or till beef is desired doneness, turning once and brushing with sauce halfway through grilling time. Add a cherry tomato to each skewer the last 1 to 2 minutes of grilling. Brush with sauce before serving.

Marinating Tips

Many of the recipes in this book call for marinating foods in a plastic bag. Use a heavy-duty bag and set it in a bowl just in case the bag leaks. There are several pluses for using a plastic bag. Usually, less marinade is needed. Distributing the marinade over the food is easy—instead of stirring the food, just turn the sealed bag occasionally. And, clean-up is simplified because the messy bag can be discarded.

If you have enough marinade, marinate foods in a glass or plastic bowl instead of a bag. Avoid using metal containers as acid in a marinade may pit the container and add an off-flavor to the marinade.

When brushing with a marinade used for meat, poultry, or fish, be sure to brush on only during the early stages of cooking. The marinade has raw meat juices in it that need to be thoroughly cooked.

Marinate foods in the refrigerator. Don't let them stand at room temperature.

Marinades are *not* reusable. Discard any leftover marinade not to be boiled and served with meat.

Per serving: 172 calories / 23 g protein / 8 g carbohydrate / 5 g fat (2 g saturated) / 65 mg cholesterol / 578 mg sodium / 579 mg potassium.

Chicken and Beef Kabobs

Indirect or Direct Grilling   Marinating Time: 2 to 4 hours   Serves 4

Marinade:	1 tablespoon finely shredded lime peel
	⅓ cup lime juice
	3 tablespoons cooking oil
	1 tablespoon toasted sesame oil
	¼ teaspoon salt
Poultry/Meat:	2 skinless, boneless, chicken breast halves (about 8 ounces total)
	8 ounces boneless beef sirloin steak, cut 1 inch thick
Vegetables:	1 small yellow summer squash *or* zucchini
	1 medium onion
	1 medium red *and/or* green sweet pepper
Glaze:	2 tablespoons honey
	1 teaspoon sesame seed

Buy 8 ounces of chicken breasts (2 halves) that are already skinned and boned. Or, select a whole, large chicken breast (about 1 pound with skin and bones) and do the work yourself. (Pictured on the cover.)

For Marinade: In a small mixing bowl combine all marinade ingredients.

To Prepare Poultry/Meat: Rinse chicken; pat dry. Trim fat from meat. Cut chicken and beef into 1-inch pieces. Place chicken and beef in a plastic bag set into a deep bowl. Pour marinade over chicken and beef in bag. Seal bag and turn chicken and beef to coat well. Marinate in the refrigerator for 2 to 4 hours, turning bag occasionally.

To Prepare Vegetables: Slice zucchini or yellow squash in half lengthwise. Then cut halves into ½-inch-thick slices. Cut onion into wedges. In a medium saucepan cook onion, covered, in a small amount of boiling water for 3 minutes. Add zucchini or squash and cook for 2 minutes more. Drain. Cut pepper into 1-inch pieces.

To Prepare Kabobs: Remove chicken and beef from bag, reserving ¼ *cup* marinade. On 8 long metal skewers, alternately thread chicken, beef, and vegetables, leaving about ¼ inch between pieces.

To Prepare Glaze: In a small mixing bowl combine ¼ cup reserved marinade, honey, and sesame seed.

To Cook by Indirect Grill Method: In a covered grill arrange preheated coals around a drip pan. Test for *medium* heat above the pan. Place kabobs on the grill rack over the drip pan. Cover and grill for 16 to 18 minutes or till chicken is tender and no longer pink, brushing with glaze after 10 minutes.

To Cook by Direct Grill Method: Grill kabobs on the grill rack of an uncovered grill directly over *medium* coals for 12 to 14 minutes or till chicken is tender and no longer pink, turning kabobs once and brushing with glaze after 6 minutes.

Per serving: 273 calories / 23 g protein / 15 g carbohydrate / 14 g fat (3 g saturated) / 62 mg cholesterol / 160 mg sodium / 410 mg potassium.

Skewered Chicken with Plum Peppercorn Vinaigrette

Indirect or Direct Grilling

Serves 4

Vinaigrette:	⅓	cup white wine vinegar
	¼	cup plum sauce
	3	tablespoons salad oil
	¼	teaspoon ground coriander
	¼	teaspoon coarsely ground black pepper
Poultry:	4	skinless, boneless, chicken breast halves (about 1 pound total)
Fruit:	4	medium plums
Vegetables:	1	cup frozen pea pods
	1	medium yellow, red, *or* green sweet pepper
	6	cups torn red-tip leaf lettuce

The vinaigrette does double duty in this main-dish salad. Use a little of it to brush on the chicken during grilling; the rest goes over the salad as a dressing.

For Vinaigrette: In a small mixing bowl combine all vinaigrette ingredients. Use *2 tablespoons* of vinaigrette as brushing sauce and reserve remainder for salad dressing.

To Prepare Poultry: Rinse chicken; pat dry. Cut chicken into 2x1-inch strips.

To Prepare Fruit: Pit plums; cut each plum into eighths.

To Prepare Vegetables: Thaw pea pods and cut in half. Cut pepper into 1-inch pieces.

To Prepare Kabobs: On 4 long metal skewers, loosely thread chicken strips accordion-style. On 4 long metal skewers, alternately thread plum and pepper pieces, leaving about ¼ inch between each.

To Cook by Indirect Grill Method: In a covered grill arrange preheated coals around a drip pan. Test for *medium* heat above the pan. Place chicken kabobs on the grill rack over the drip pan. Cover and grill for 10 to 12 minutes or till chicken is tender and no longer pink, turning once and brushing occasionally with reserved vinaigrette. Place plum and pepper kabobs beside the chicken kabobs on the grill rack. Grill directly over *medium-hot* coals the last 3 minutes of grilling or till heated through.

To Cook by Direct Grill Method: Grill chicken kabobs on the grill rack of an uncovered grill directly over *medium* coals for 10 to 12 minutes or till chicken is tender and no longer pink, turning once and brushing occasionally with reserved vinaigrette. Place the plum and pepper kabobs beside the chicken kabobs on the grill rack. Grill directly over *medium* coals the last 3 minutes of grilling or till heated through.

To Serve: Divide the leaf lettuce among 4 dinner plates. Top with skewered chicken, plum and pepper pieces, and pea pods. Serve with reserved plum vinaigrette.

Per serving: 314 calories / 26 g protein / 24 g carbohydrate / 15 g fat (2 g saturated) / 59 mg cholesterol / 74 mg sodium / 658 mg potassium.

Breakfast-on-a-Stick

Breakfast-on-a-Stick

Indirect or Direct Grilling Serves 4

Bread:	⅓ cup sugar
	1½ teaspoons ground cinnamon
	4 brown-and-serve rolls, quartered
	¼ cup margarine *or* butter, melted
Meat:	8 ounces sliced Canadian-style bacon
Fruit:	Kiwi fruit, orange, *or* banana pieces *or* strawberries

Fold the Canadian-style bacon slices into quarters and thread them onto the skewers so that they won't unfold.

To Prepare Bread: In a small mixing bowl combine sugar and cinnamon. Brush the quartered rolls with the melted margarine or butter and then sprinkle with the sugar-cinnamon mixture, turning to coat all sides.

To Prepare Kabobs: On 4 long metal skewers, alternately thread bread and bacon that has been folded in quarters, leaving about ¼ inch between pieces.

To Cook by Indirect Grill Method: In a covered grill arrange preheated coals around a drip pan. Test for *low* heat above the pan. Place kabobs on the grill rack over the drip pan. Cover and grill for 10 to 12 minutes or till heated through.

To Cook by Direct Grill Method: Grill kabobs on the grill rack of an uncovered grill directly over *low* coals, avoiding direct flame, for 8 to 10 minutes or till heated through, turning once.

To Serve: Thread a piece of kiwi fruit, orange, or banana or a whole strawberry on the end of each kabob before serving.

Per serving: 330 calories / 11 g protein / 35 g carbohydrate / 17 g fat (4 g saturated) / 21 mg cholesterol / 830 mg sodium / 233 mg potassium.

Singapore Satay

Indirect or Direct Grilling | Marinating Time: 1 to 2 hours | Serves 4

Marinade:	¼	cup soy sauce
	2	tablespoons cooking oil
	2	tablespoons lemon juice
	1	tablespoon toasted sesame oil
	1	tablespoon honey
	1	teaspoon curry powder
	1	clove garlic, minced
Meat:	12	ounces lean boneless pork
Sauce:	4	to 5 tablespoons hot water
	¼	cup peanut butter
	1	small green onion, chopped
	½	teaspoon grated gingerroot
		Dash ground red pepper
Rice:	2	cups hot cooked rice

When buying pork for this recipe, consider using a boneless pork loin chop, cut 1 to 1¼ inch thick.

For Marinade: In a small mixing bowl combine all marinade ingredients.

To Prepare Meat: Trim fat from meat. Cut meat into long slices about ¼ inch thick. Place pork in a plastic bag set into a deep bowl. Pour marinade over pork in bag. Seal bag and turn pork to coat well. Marinate in the refrigerator for 1 to 2 hours, turning bag occasionally.

For Sauce: In a small bowl gradually stir hot water into peanut butter till smooth and of a sauce consistency. Stir in green onion, gingerroot, and red pepper. Set aside.

To Prepare Kabobs: Remove pork from bag, reserving marinade. On 4 long metal skewers, thread pork slices, leaving about ¼ inch between pieces.

To Cook by Indirect Grill Method: In a covered grill arrange preheated coals around a drip pan. Test for *medium* heat above the pan. Place kabobs on the grill rack over the drip pan. Cover and grill for 12 to 14 minutes or till pork is done and juices run clear, brushing with reserved marinade halfway through grilling time.

To Cook by Direct Grill Method: Grill kabobs on the grill rack of an uncovered grill directly over *medium* coals for 10 to 12 minutes or till pork is done and juices run clear, turning once and brushing with reserved marinade halfway through grilling time.

To Serve: Place kabobs over cooked rice. Serve with sauce.

Per serving: 388 calories / 19 g protein / 36 g carbohydrate / 19 g fat (4 g saturated) / 38 mg cholesterol / 623 mg sodium / 340 mg potassium.

Pork and Vegetable Kabobs

Indirect or Direct Grilling	Marinating Time: 2 to 4 hours	Serves 4

Marinade:	½ of a 6-ounce can (⅓ cup) frozen apple juice concentrate, thawed
	2 tablespoons white wine vinegar
	2 tablespoons olive oil *or* cooking oil
	2 tablespoons soy sauce
	½ teaspoon dried savory, crushed
	¼ teaspoon pepper
Meat:	1 pound lean boneless pork
Vegetables:	2 cups broccoli flowerets
	2 medium carrots, cut into 1-inch chunks

The apple juice lends a sweetness, the vinegar adds a tang, and the broccoli and carrots add lots of color to these kabobs.

For Marinade: In a small mixing bowl combine all marinade ingredients.

To Prepare Meat: Trim fat from meat. Cut pork into 1-inch cubes. Place pork in a plastic bag set into a deep bowl. Pour marinade over pork in bag. Seal bag and turn pork to coat well. Marinate in the refrigerator for 2 to 4 hours, turning bag occasionally.

To Prepare Vegetables: In a medium saucepan cook carrots, covered, in small amount of boiling water for 3 minutes. Add broccoli and cook for 1 to 2 minutes more or till crisp-tender. Drain.

To Prepare Kabobs: Remove pork from bag, reserving marinade. On 4 long metal skewers, alternately thread pork, broccoli, and carrots, leaving about ¼ inch between pieces.

To Cook by Indirect Grill Method: In a covered grill arrange preheated coals around a drip pan. Test for *medium* heat above the pan. Place kabobs on the grill rack over the drip pan. Cover and grill for 16 to 18 minutes or till pork is tender and juices run clear, brushing with reserved marinade halfway through grilling time.

To Cook by Direct Grill Method: Grill kabobs on the grill rack of an uncovered grill directly over *medium* coals for 12 to 14 minutes or till pork is tender and juices run clear, turning once and brushing with reserved marinade halfway through cooking time.

Per serving: 281 calories / 19 g protein / 20 g carbohydrate / 15 g fat (4 g saturated) / 51 mg cholesterol / 604 mg sodium / 637 mg potassium.

Rumaki-Style Scallop Kabobs

Rumaki-Style Scallop Kabobs

Indirect or Direct Grilling   Marinating Time: 1 to 2 hours   Serves 4

Marinade:	½ cup dry white wine
	¼ cup olive oil *or* cooking oil
	¼ cup lemon juice
	1 tablespoon Dijon-style mustard
	¼ teaspoon pepper
Seafood:	1 pound fresh *or* frozen sea scallops (thawed, if frozen)
Vegetables:	2 medium yellow summer squash *or* zucchini
Meat:	4 ounces thinly sliced prosciutto *or* fully cooked ham
	Fresh basil leaves (about 32)
Garnish:	Tomatoes, cut in wedges

Fresh basil leaves add a unique flavor to these kabobs. Cut fresh leaves from the garden or look for fresh basil in the produce department of your supermarket. If desired, serve the kabobs with rice pilaf.

For Marinade: In a small mixing bowl combine all marinade ingredients.

To Prepare Seafood: Cut any large scallops in half. Place scallops in a plastic bag set into a deep bowl. Pour marinade over scallops in bag. Seal bag and turn scallops to coat well. Marinate in the refrigerator for 1 to 2 hours, turning bag occasionally.

To Prepare Vegetables: Cut yellow squash or zucchini into ½-inch-thick slices. In a medium saucepan cook squash, covered, in a small amount of boiling water for 2 minutes. Drain. Set aside.

To Prepare Meat: Cut prosciutto or ham into 1-inch-wide strips.

To Prepare Kabobs: Remove scallops from bag, reserving marinade. Place a basil leaf on each scallop; wrap with a strip of meat. On 8 long metal skewers, alternately thread the wrapped scallops and squash, leaving about ¼ inch between pieces.

To Cook by Indirect Grill Method: In a covered grill arrange preheated coals around a drip pan. Test for *medium* heat above the pan. Place kabobs on the greased grill rack over the drip pan. Cover and grill for 13 to 15 minutes or till scallops turn opaque, brushing with reserved marinade halfway through grilling time.

To Cook by Direct Grill Method: Grill kabobs on the greased rack of an uncovered grill directly over *medium* coals for 10 to 12 minutes or till scallops turn opaque, turning once and brushing with reserved marinade halfway through grilling time.

To Serve: Serve the kabobs on plates garnished with tomato wedges.

Per serving: 255 calories / 23 g protein / 6 g carbohydrate / 15 g fat (1 g saturated) / 34 mg cholesterol / 721 mg sodium / 529 mg potassium.

Shrimp-Salmon Kabobs

Indirect Grilling   Marinating Time: 2 to 4 hours   Serves 4

Marinade:	¼	cup wine vinegar
	¼	cup catsup
	2	tablespoons cooking oil
	2	tablespoons soy sauce
	1	teaspoon prepared mustard
	1	clove garlic, minced
	¼	teaspoon pepper
Vegetables:	2	small zucchini or yellow summer squash
	2	cups fresh pea pods or small whole fresh mushrooms
Seafood:	12	ounces fresh or frozen large shrimp in shells (about 16) (thawed, if frozen)
	8	ounces fresh or frozen salmon fillet, cut 1 inch thick (thawed, if frozen)

If fresh pea pods are not available, use the mushrooms or 2 medium red sweet peppers instead. Cut the red peppers into 1-inch pieces.

For Marinade: In a small mixing bowl combine all marinade ingredients.

To Prepare Seafood: Peel and devein shrimp, keeping tails intact. Cut salmon into 1-inch pieces. Place seafood and vegetables in a plastic bag set into a deep bowl. Pour marinade over seafood and vegetables in bag. Seal bag and turn seafood and vegetables to coat well. Marinate in the refrigerator for 2 to 4 hours, turning bag occasionally.

To Prepare Vegetables: Cut zucchini or summer squash into ½-inch-thick slices. In a medium saucepan cook zucchini or summer squash, covered, in a small amount of boiling water for 1 to 2 minutes or till nearly tender. Drain and cool. Remove tips and strings from pea pods. Set all vegetables aside.

To Prepare Kabobs: Remove seafood and vegetables from bag, reserving marinade. On 8 long metal skewers, alternately thread seafood and vegetables, leaving about ¼ inch between the pieces.

To Cook by Indirect Grill Method: In a covered grill arrange preheated coals around a drip pan. Test for *medium* heat above the pan. Place kabobs on the greased grill rack over the drip pan. Cover and grill for 6 to 8 minutes or till shrimp turn opaque and salmon just flakes with a fork, brushing with reserved marinade halfway through grilling time.

Per serving: 204 calories / 25 g protein / 12 g carbohydrate / 7 g fat (1 g saturated) / 141 mg cholesterol / 854 mg sodium / 538 mg potassium.

SOME SPECIAL EXTRAS

■

As long as the fire is going for your entrée, why not add

a few extras to the grill? You might be surprised

at the possibilities—Grilled German Potato Salad,

Southwestern Grilled Corn, Carrot-Dill Bread,

and Caramel Apple Slices to name a fabulous few.

Summer Vegetables

Direct Grilling   Serves 8

Vegetables:	2 pounds asparagus spears, baby carrots, eggplant, fennel, leeks, sweet peppers, new potatoes, scallopini squash, *and/or* baby zucchini *or* regular zucchini
Brush-on:	¼ cup olive oil, melted margarine, *or* melted butter

The nutrition information varies with the vegetables selected, from 74 calories for ¼ pound of zucchini to 172 calories for ¼ pound of potatoes. The nutrition information following this recipe is based on a combination of asparagus, carrots, leeks, zucchini, summer squash, and sweet pepper.

To Prepare Vegetables: Before grilling, rinse, trim, cut up, and precook vegetables as directed in the chart on page 234. Generously brush vegetables with olive oil, margarine, or butter before grilling. Grill vegetables according to the chart, turning occasionally.

Per serving with vegetable assortment: 92 calories / 1 g protein / 7 g carbohydrate / 7 g fat (1 g saturated) / 0 mg cholesterol / 18 mg sodium / 225 mg potassium.

Vegetable Medley with Macadamia Nut Butter

Direct Grilling   Serves 8

Nut Butter:	¼ cup margarine *or* butter
	2 tablespoons ground macadamia nuts *or* almonds
	2 tablespoons walnut, almond, *or* olive oil
	1 tablespoon snipped cilantro *or* parsley
Vegetables:	2 pounds asparagus, baby carrots, eggplant, fennel, sweet peppers, leeks, new potatoes, *and/or* zucchini *or* yellow summer squash, cut into 1-inch-thick slices
	Salt
	Pepper

The nutrition information for this recipe is based on a combination of asparagus, eggplant, leeks, zucchini, and summer squash.

For Nut Butter: In a small saucepan combine all nut butter ingredients. Cook and stir over medium heat for 5 to 6 minutes or till nuts are toasted, stirring occasionally.

To Prepare Vegetables: Before grilling, rinse, trim, cut up, and precook vegetables as directed in the chart on page 234. Grill vegetables according to the chart, *except* brush occasionally with nut butter instead of the olive oil, margarine, or butter. Sprinkle grilled vegetables with salt and pepper.

Per serving with vegetable assortment: 126 calories / 2 g protein / 7 g carbohydrate / 11 g fat (2 g saturated) / 0 mg cholesterol / 140 mg sodium / 245 mg potassium.

Summer Vegetables

Summer Squash Casserole

Direct Grilling   Serves 8

Vegetables:	2	pounds yellow summer squash *and/or* zucchini
	¼	cup chopped onion
	1	10¾-ounce can condensed cream of chicken soup
	1	8-ounce carton dairy sour cream
	2	medium carrots, shredded (about 1 cup)
Bread Mixture:	½	of an 8-ounce package (2 cups) herb-seasoned stuffing mix
	¼	cup margarine *or* butter, melted

Do you have a grill that's too small to cook both the large vegetable packet and the turkey recipe suggested on page 67? Then make 2 smaller packets to put on each side of the grill next to the bird. For the smaller packets, make a double thickness of foil using two 18x18-inch pieces of heavy foil.

To Prepare Vegetables: Slice yellow squash and/or zucchini in half lengthwise. Then cut halves into ½-inch-thick slices (about 7 cups). Cook the yellow squash and/or zucchini and onion, covered, in a small amount of boiling water about 3 minutes or till crisp-tender. Drain well. In an extra-large mixing bowl stir together soup, sour cream, and carrots. Stir in squash and onion. Set aside.

To Prepare Bread Mixture: In a medium mixing bowl toss the stuffing mix with the melted margarine or butter.

To Prepare Packet: Tear off two 24x18-inch pieces of heavy foil. Make a double thickness of foil that measures 24x18 inches. Arrange *half* of the bread mixture on the foil in a 12x7-inch rectangle. Spoon vegetable mixture over bread mixture on foil. Top with remaining bread mixture. Bring up two opposite edges of foil and seal with a double fold. Then fold remaining ends to completely enclose the mixture, leaving space for steam to build.

To Cook by Direct Grill Method: Grill foil packet on the grill rack of a grill directly over *medium* to *medium-high* coals about 20 minutes or till heated through.

Per serving: 233 calories / 5 g protein / 21 g carbohydrate / 15 g fat (6 g saturated) / 16 mg cholesterol / 694 mg sodium / 337 mg potassium.

Grilled German Potato Salad

Direct Grilling   Serves 4

Vegetable:	3 medium potatoes (about 1 pound), cut into ¾-inch cubes
Dressing:	4 slices bacon
	1 medium onion, chopped (½ cup)
	½ cup finely chopped celery
	1 tablespoon all-purpose flour
	1 tablespoon sugar
	½ teaspoon salt
	½ teaspoon celery seed
	¼ teaspoon dry mustard
	⅛ teaspoon pepper
	⅓ cup water
	¼ cup cider vinegar

Heat this salad favorite alongside meat or poultry as it cooks. It goes great with sausages, chops, steaks, burgers, or chicken pieces. (Pictured on page 46.)

To Prepare Vegetable: In a large covered saucepan cook the potatoes in a small amount of boiling lightly salted water for 10 minutes. Drain potatoes well; cool slightly. Set aside.

For Dressing: In a large skillet cook bacon till crisp. Drain the bacon, reserving *2 tablespoons* of the drippings. Crumble bacon; set aside. Cook onion and celery in the reserved drippings till tender. Stir in flour, sugar, salt, celery seed, mustard, and pepper. Add water and vinegar all at once. Cook and stir till thickened and bubbly. Remove from heat. Stir in crumbled bacon.

To Prepare Packet: Tear off a 36x18-inch piece of heavy foil. Fold in half to make a double thickness of foil that measures 18x18 inches. Place potatoes in the center of the foil. Pour dressing over potatoes. Bring up two opposite edges of foil and seal with a double fold. Then fold remaining ends to completely enclose the potato mixture, leaving space for steam to build.

To Cook by Direct Grill Method: Grill foil packet on the grill rack of a grill directly over *medium* to *medium-high* coals for 15 to 20 minutes or till heated through.

Per serving: 243 calories / 5 g protein / 35 g carbohydrate / 10 g fat (4 g saturated) / 11 mg cholesterol / 391 mg sodium / 633 mg potassium.

Apricot and Brown Rice Pilaf

Direct Grilling   Serves 4

Rice Mixture:	
2	cups chicken broth
1	cup regular brown rice
2	green onions, sliced (¼ cup)
¼	cup snipped dried apricots
¼	teaspoon pepper
¼	cup slivered almonds, toasted

Make this recipe to go along with grilled chicken pieces (see recipe, page 49). Or add the pilaf packet to the side of the grill when cooking pork chops or lamb.

For Rice Mixture: In a medium saucepan combine chicken broth, rice, green onions, apricots, and pepper. Bring to boiling; reduce heat. Cover and simmer about 35 minutes or till rice is tender. Stir in almonds.

To Prepare Packet: Tear off a 36x18-inch piece of heavy foil. Fold in half to make a double thickness of foil that measures 18x18 inches. Place pilaf in the center of the foil. Bring up two opposite edges of foil and seal with a double fold. Then fold remaining ends to completely enclose the pilaf, leaving space for steam to build.

To Cook by Direct Grill Method: Grill foil packet on the grill rack of a grill directly over *medium* to *medium-high* coals about 20 minutes or till pilaf is heated through, turning packet frequently.

Foil-Wrapped Side Dishes

Preparing side dishes in foil packets is a slick trick that helps you make the best use of your grill. Place the packet alongside the meat as it cooks. If the meat takes longer to cook than the packet, keep the prepared packet in the refrigerator until it's time to add it to the grill. You may need to add a few extra minutes of grilling time to make sure that the chilled side dish is thoroughly heated. After grilling, be sure to open the foil packets carefully—the steam that builds in the sealed package is very hot.

Per serving: 253 calories / 8 g protein / 43 g carbohydrate / 6 g fat (1 g saturated) / 0 mg cholesterol / 393 mg sodium / 381 mg potassium.

Walnut-Bulgur Pilaf

Direct Grilling   Serves 4

Bulgur Mixture:	1⅓	cups water
	1	tablespoon olive oil *or* cooking oil
	1	tablespoon lemon juice
	1	teaspoon instant chicken bouillon granules
	½	teaspoon dried oregano, crushed
	⅛	teaspoon pepper
	¾	cup bulgur
	4	green onions, sliced (½ cup)
	1	clove garlic, minced
Toppings:	1	medium tomato, chopped
	¼	cup chopped walnuts

Accompany the Greek Kabobs (see recipe, page 154) with this pilaf mixture. Or, serve it as a side dish with grilled fish.

For Bulgur Mixture: In a medium saucepan combine water, olive oil or cooking oil, lemon juice, bouillon granules, oregano, and pepper. Bring to boiling. Add bulgur, green onions, and garlic. Cover and simmer for 10 minutes. Remove from heat.

To Prepare Packet: Tear off a 36x18-inch piece of heavy foil. Fold in half to make a double thickness of foil that measures 18x18-inches. Place bulgur mixture in the center of the foil. Bring up two opposite edges of foil and seal with a double fold. Then fold remaining ends to completely enclose the bulgur mixture, leaving space for steam to build.

To Cook by Direct Grill Method: Grill foil packet on the grill rack of a grill directly over *medium* to *medium-high* coals for 8 to 10 minutes or till pilaf is heated through, turning packet frequently.

To Serve: Carefully open packet. Stir tomatoes and walnuts into the bulgur mixture.

Per serving: 179 calories / 5 g protein / 24 g carbohydrate / 9 g fat (1 g saturated) / 0 mg cholesterol / 227 mg sodium / 240 mg potassium.

Grilled Vegetable Packet

Grilled Vegetable Packet

Direct Grilling   Serves 4

Seasoning:	¼	cup margarine *or* butter
	¼	teaspoon salt
	¼	teaspoon pepper
Vegetables:	1½	pounds tiny new potatoes, sliced
	4	medium carrots, sliced
	1	medium onion, sliced
	1	medium green pepper, cut into strips

Give this recipe a try when you're looking for a basic buttered vegetable to serve with grilled meat, poultry, or fish.

For Seasoning: In a small saucepan melt margarine or butter. Stir in salt and pepper. Set aside.

To Prepare Vegetables: Toss potatoes, carrots, onion, and pepper together.

To Prepare Packet: Tear off a 36x18-inch piece of heavy foil. Fold in half to make a double thickness of foil that measures 18x18 inches. Place the vegetables in the center of the foil. Drizzle seasoning mixture over

vegetables. Bring up two opposite edges of foil and seal with a double fold. Then fold remaining ends to completely enclose the vegetables, leaving space for steam to build.

To Cook by Direct Grill Method: Grill the foil packet on the grill rack of a grill directly over *medium* to *medium-high* coals for 35 to 45 minutes or till potatoes and carrots are tender.

Per serving: 315 calories / 5 g protein / 50 g carbohydrate / 12 g fat (2 g saturated) / 0 mg cholesterol / 326 mg sodium / 917 mg potassium.

Artichoke Hearts and Mushrooms

Direct Grilling   Serves 4

Vegetables:	12	pearl onions
	12	large mushrooms (about 1½- to 2-inch diameter)
	1	9-ounce package frozen artichoke hearts, thawed
Sauce:	2	tablespoons cooking oil
	1	tablespoon white wine Worcestershire sauce
	1	tablespoon Dijon-style mustard

Looking for an elegant side dish to dress up a grilled steak or some poultry? Here is one suggestion to serve to your guests.

To Prepare Vegetables: In a medium saucepan cook the onions, covered, in a small amount of boiling water for 3 minutes. Add mushrooms; cover and cook for 1 minute more. Drain. Cool slightly.

To Prepare Kabobs: On 4 to 6 long metal skewers, alternately thread onions, mushrooms, and artichoke hearts, leaving about ¼ inch between pieces.

For Sauce: In a small mixing bowl combine all sauce ingredients. Brush sauce over all sides of kabobs.

To Cook by Direct Grill Method: Grill kabobs on the grill rack of a grill directly over *medium* to *medium-high* coals about 4 minutes or till vegetables are heated through, turning once and brushing with sauce.

Per serving: 120 calories / 4 g protein / 12 g carbohydrate / 7 g fat (1 g saturated) / 0 mg cholesterol / 189 mg sodium / 430 mg potassium.

Lemony Grilled Turnips

Direct Grilling

Serves 4

Seasoning:	2 tablespoons olive oil *or* cooking oil
	½ teaspoon finely shredded lemon peel
	2 tablespoons lemon juice
	½ teaspoon dried thyme, crushed
	¼ teaspoon salt
	¼ teaspoon pepper
Vegetable:	3 medium turnips (about 1 pound total), peeled

Grilled turnips offer a tasty change of pace from potatoes. Turnips are round, root vegetables with a white and purple skin and creamy white meat.

For Seasoning: In a small mixing bowl stir together all seasoning ingredients. Set aside.

To Prepare Vegetables: Cut the turnips into ¾-inch-thick slices. In a medium saucepan cook turnips in a small amount of boiling lightly salted water for 8 minutes or till nearly tender. Drain. Tear off a 24x18-inch piece of heavy foil. Fold in half to make a double thickness of foil that measures 12x18 inches. Place sliced turnips on foil.

To Cook by Direct Grill Method: Place foil with turnips on the grill rack of a grill directly over *medium* to *medium-high* coals about 20 minutes or till tender, turning turnips once halfway through grilling time and brushing occasionally with seasoning mixture.

Per serving: 82 calories / 1 g protein / 6 g carbohydrate / 7 g fat (1 g saturated) / 0 mg cholesterol / 187 mg sodium / 158 mg potassium.

Southwestern Grilled Corn

Direct Grilling   Serves 6

Seasoning:	⅓ cup margarine *or* butter
	2 tablespoons snipped cilantro *or* parsley
	¼ teaspoon salt
	¼ teaspoon ground red pepper
Vegetable:	6 fresh ears of corn

Remember to turn the foil-wrapped ears as they grill to get corn that's evenly cooked. For those who like more seasoning, sprinkle corn with additional salt and red pepper to taste.

For Seasoning: In a small saucepan melt margarine or butter. Stir in cilantro or parsley, salt, and ground red pepper.

To Prepare Vegetable: Remove the husks from fresh ears of corn. Scrub ears with a stiff brush to remove silks. Rinse ears; pat dry with paper towels. Place each ear of corn on a piece of heavy foil. Brush ears with seasoning mixture. Wrap corn securely in foil.

To Cook by Direct Grill Method: Grill corn on the grill rack of a grill directly over *medium* to *medium-high* coals about 20 minutes or till kernels are tender, turning frequently.

Per serving: 173 calories / 3 g protein / 19 g carbohydrate / 11 g fat (2 g saturated) / 0 mg cholesterol / 220 mg sodium / 201 mg potassium.

Southwestern Grilled Corn

Grilled Tomatoes with Pesto

Indirect Grilling   Serves 6

Vegetables:	3	medium tomatoes
	2	tablespoons purchased pesto sauce
	6	very thin onion slices
Topping:	½	cup shredded Monterey Jack cheese (2 ounces)
	⅓	cup smoked *or* toasted almonds, chopped
	2	tablespoons snipped parsley
Seasonings:		Salt
		Pepper
Garnish:		Parsley sprigs

Smoked almonds add to the distinctive flavor of this side dish. Look for these nuts in the snack section of your supermarket. (Pictured on page 144.)

To Prepare Vegetables: Let tomatoes come to room temperature. Remove cores from tomatoes and cut tomatoes in half crosswise. Using a spoon, hollow out the top ¼ inch of the tomato halves. Top *each* tomato half with *1 teaspoon* of pesto sauce and *1* onion slice. Arrange the tomato halves in 2 foil pie pans. Set aside.

For Topping: In a small mixing bowl stir together all topping ingredients. Set aside.

To Cook by Indirect Grill Method: In a covered grill arrange preheated coals for indirect grilling. Test for *medium* heat where tomatoes will cook. Place foil pans containing the tomatoes on the grill rack not over the coals. Cover and grill for 10 to 15 minutes or till tomatoes halves are heated through. Sprinkle topping over tomatoes. Cover and grill about 5 minutes more or till cheese is melted. Season to taste with salt and pepper. If desired, garnish with parsley sprigs.

Per serving: 131 calories / 5 g protein / 6 g carbohydrate / 10 g fat (2 g saturated) / 9 mg cholesterol / 119 sodium / 218 mg potassium.

Herbed Sourdough Bread

Direct Grilling   Serves 12

Spread:	½	cup margarine *or* butter, softened
	2	tablespoons snipped chives *or* finely chopped green onion
	2	tablespoons snipped parsley
	4	teaspoons snipped fresh tarragon *or* ¾ teaspoon dried tarragon, crushed
Bread:	1	16-ounce loaf unsliced sourdough bread

For make-ahead convenience, assemble, wrap, and refrigerate this bread ahead of time. About 15 minutes before serving, add the foil-wrapped package to the grill and heat through.

For Spread: In a small mixing bowl stir together all spread ingredients.

For Bread: Cut bread crosswise into 1-inch-thick slices, *cutting to but not through* bottom crust. Spread cut surfaces with spread. Tear off a 48x18-inch piece of heavy foil. Fold in half to make a double thickness of foil that measures 24x18 inches. Place bread in the center of the foil. Bring up two opposite edges of foil and seal with a double fold. Then fold remaining ends to completely enclose the bread, leaving space for steam to build.

To Cook by Direct Grill Method: Grill bread on the grill rack of a grill directly over *medium* to *medium-high* coals about 15 minutes or till heated through.

Per serving: 174 calories / 4 g protein / 19 g carbohydrate / 9 g fat (2 g saturated) / 0 mg cholesterol / 298 mg sodium / 43 mg potassium.

Carrot-Dill Bread

Indirect Grilling   Serves 16

Dough:	1	16-ounce package hot roll mix
	1	cup whole wheat flour
	1	medium carrot, shredded (½ cup)
	2	tablespoon snipped fresh dill *or* 2 teaspoons dried dillweed
	1⅓	cups warm water (120° to 130°)
	1	egg
	2	tablespoons margarine *or* butter, softened
Topping:	1	beaten egg
	1	tablespoon water

Bake a loaf of bread on the barbecue grill instead of heating up your kitchen with indoor baking.

To Prepare Dough: In a large mixing bowl combine flour mixture and packet of yeast from hot roll mix. Stir in whole wheat flour, carrot, and dill. Add warm water, egg, and margarine or butter. Stir till mixture forms a moderately stiff dough. Knead dough on a lightly floured surface for 5 minutes, adding a little more flour as needed. Shape dough into a round loaf. Place dough in a greased 9x1½-inch round baking pan. Flatten to an 8-inch diameter. Cover; let rise in a warm place till double (20 to 30 minutes).

For Topping: Combine the beaten egg and water; brush over loaf. With a very sharp knife, make 3 cuts, about ¼ inch deep, across the top of the loaf. Make 3 additional shallow cuts, forming a diamond pattern in top of loaf.

To Cook by Indirect Grill Method: In a covered grill arrange preheated coals for indirect grilling. Test for *medium* heat where bread will bake. Place baking pan on the grill rack not over coals. Cover and grill for 30 to 35 minutes or till bread tests done and crust is golden. Makes 16 servings.

Per serving: 154 calories / 6 g protein / 27 g carbohydrate / 3 g fat (0 g saturated) / 27 mg cholesterol / 192 mg sodium / 107 mg potassium.

Carrot-Dill Bread

French Bread with Roasted Garlic

Direct Grilling		Serves 16
Seasoning:	2 whole heads of garlic	
	½ cup olive oil _or_ cooking oil	
	1 tablespoon snipped fresh basil, oregano, rosemary, _or_ thyme	
Bread:	1 16-ounce loaf unsliced French bread	

Attention, garlic lovers! Nearly two dozen cloves (equivalent to two whole heads of garlic) are spread over toasted French bread slices for a pungent side dish.

For Seasoning: Remove the papery outer layers from the garlic heads. Tear off two 18x18-inch pieces of heavy foil. Fold each piece in half to make a double thickness of foil that measures 9x18 inches. Place _one_ head of garlic on the center of _each_ piece of foil. Bring the foil up around the garlic on all sides forming a cup. Pour ¼ _cup_ of the oil over _each_ head of garlic, letting the oil flow between the cloves and onto the bottom of the cup. Sprinkle _each_ with _half_ of the herb. Twist the sides of the foil to completely enclose the garlic heads in the foil.

For Bread: Cut French bread into 1-inch-thick slices.

To Cook by Direct Grill Method: Grill foil packets on the grill rack of a grill directly over _medium_ to _medium-high_ coals for 25 minutes. Add the bread slices to the grill rack. Grill for 2 to 4 minutes more or till the bread is toasted and garlic cloves are tender, turning bread once.

To Serve: Transfer garlic heads to a plate; pour any oil in the foil over the garlic. For each serving, brush a slice of bread with some of the herbed oil. Break off a clove of garlic and squeeze the paste from the garlic clove onto the bread and spread over bread.

Per serving: 145 calories / 3 g protein / 16 g carbohydrate / 8 g fat (1 g saturated) / 0 mg cholesterol / 158 mg sodium / 42 mg potassium.

Grilled Cherry Dessert

Indirect Grilling   Serves 4 to 6

Fruit Mixture:	4 cups fresh *or* frozen unsweetened pitted tart red cherries (partially thawed, if frozen)
	⅔ cup sugar
	2 tablespoons water
	1 tablespoon cornstarch
Topping:	½ cup quick-cooking oats
	½ cup packed brown sugar
	¼ cup all-purpose flour
	½ teaspoon ground nutmeg *or* cinnamon
	¼ cup margarine *or* butter
Accompaniment:	Vanilla ice cream

Put the dessert on the grill to cook while you're enjoying the rest of the meal. Then, spoon the warm cherry mixture over scoops of ice cream. A ¼-cup serving of ice cream is included in the nutrition information.

For Fruit: In a medium saucepan combine all fruit mixture ingredients. Cook and stir till thickened and bubbly. Transfer mixture to an 8x8x2-inch metal baking or foil pan. Set fruit mixture aside.

For Topping: In a medium mixing bowl combine oats, brown sugar, flour, and nutmeg or cinnamon. Cut in margarine or butter till mixture resembles coarse crumbs. Sprinkle topping over cherry mixture in pan.

To Cook by Indirect Grill Method: In a covered grill arrange preheated coals for indirect cooking. Test for *medium* heat where dessert will cook. Place dessert on the grill rack not over the coals. Cover and grill for 25 to 30 minutes or till topping is set.

To Serve: Serve cherry dessert over scoops of ice cream.

Per serving: 537 calories / 5 g protein / 98 g carbohydrate / 17 g fat (5 g saturated) / 15 mg cholesterol / 174 mg sodium / 401 mg potassium.

Chocolate-Sauced Dessert Kabobs

Chocolate-Sauced Dessert Kabobs

Direct Grilling   Serves 6

Sauce:	¾ cup semisweet chocolate pieces
	¼ cup margarine *or* butter
	⅔ cup sugar
	1 5-ounce can (⅔ cup) evaporated milk
Kabobs:	2 medium ripe nectarines *or* peaches
	2 ripe bananas
	½ of a 10¾-ounce frozen loaf pound cake
	6 whole strawberries

Leftover chocolate sauce makes a tasty topping for ice cream. Store it, covered, in the refrigerator.

For Sauce: In a heavy small saucepan melt chocolate pieces and margarine or butter over low heat. Add the sugar. Gradually stir in milk. Bring to boiling; reduce heat. Boil gently over low heat for 8 minutes, stirring frequently. Remove from heat. Set aside.

To Prepare Kabobs: Peel peaches, if using. Remove pits from nectarines or peaches; cut fruit into wedges. Cut the bananas into 1-inch pieces. Cut the cake into 1-inch cubes. Remove stems from strawberries. On 6 long skewers, alternately thread peaches or nectarines, bananas, and cake cubes. Add one strawberry to each skewer.

To Cook by Direct Grill Method: Grill kabobs on the grill rack directly over *medium* coals about 5 minutes or till cake is toasted, turning once.

To Serve: For each serving, push fruit and cake from skewers onto a dessert plate. Drizzle with chocolate sauce. (Store any remaining sauce tightly covered in the refrigerator for another use.)

Per serving: 455 calories / 5 g protein / 63 g carbohydrate / 23 g fat (7 g saturated) / 59 mg cholesterol / 162 mg sodium / 393 mg potassium.

Caramel Apple Slices

Indirect or Direct Grilling — Serves 4 to 6

Topping:	⅓	cup packed brown sugar
	2	tablespoons margarine *or* butter, softened
	2	tablespoons light corn syrup
	1	teaspoon ground cinnamon
Fruit:	3	cups sliced, peeled cooking apples (3 medium)
Accompaniment:	1	pint vanilla ice cream

Want an apple sundae? Just spoon the grilled apples and sauce over scoops of vanilla ice cream.

For Topping: In a small mixing bowl stir together all topping ingredients; set aside.

To Prepare Packet: Tear off a 36x18-inch piece of heavy foil. Fold in half to make a double thickness of foil that measures 18x18 inches. Place apples in the center of the foil. Drizzle with topping. Bring up two opposite edges of foil and seal with a double fold. Then fold remaining ends to completely enclose the apples, leaving space for steam to build.

To Cook by Indirect Grill Method: In a covered grill arrange preheated coals for indirect grilling. Test for *medium* heat where apples will cook. Place foil packet on grill rack not over coals. Cover and grill for 30 to 35 minutes or till apples are tender.

To Cook by Direct Grill Method: Grill foil packet on the grill rack of an uncovered grill directly over *medium* coals for 15 to 20 minutes or till apples are tender.

To Serve: Serve apple mixture warm with ice cream.

Per serving: 353 calories / 3 g protein / 59 g carbohydrate / 13 g fat (6 g saturated) / 30 mg cholesterol / 139 mg sodium / 310 mg potassium.

Three-Way Chicken Wings

Indirect or Direct Grilling   Serves 8

Easy Barbecue Sauce:	1	cup chili sauce
	½	cup currant jelly, melted
	2	tablespoons snipped chives
	2	teaspoons prepared mustard
Spicy Mustard Sauce:	1⅓	cups chicken broth
	½	cup hot-style mustard
	4	teaspoons cornstarch
	2	teaspoons soy sauce
Sweet-and-Sour Sauce:	⅔	cup packed brown sugar
	⅔	cup unsweetened pineapple juice
	⅔	cup red wine vinegar
	2	tablespoons cornstarch
	2	tablespoons soy sauce
	¼	teaspoon ground ginger
Chicken:	24	chicken wings (about 4½ pounds)

Brush the chicken pieces with one of three sauces the last 5 minutes of grilling so that the sauce doesn't burn.

For Easy Barbecue Sauce: In a small mixing bowl stir together all the ingredients. Makes 1½ cups.

For Spicy Mustard Sauce: In a small saucepan stir together all the ingredients. Cook and stir till thickened and bubbly. Cook and stir for 2 minutes more. Makes 1⅓ cups.

For Sweet-and-Sour Sauce: In a small saucepan stir together all the ingredients. Cook and stir till thickened and bubbly. Cook and stir for 2 minutes more. Makes 1⅓ cups.

To Prepare Chicken: Rinse chicken wings; pat dry. Tuck wing tips under.

To Cook by Indirect Grill Method: In a covered grill arrange preheated coals around a drip pan. Test for *medium* heat above the pan. Place chicken wings on the grill rack over the drip pan. Cover and grill for 25 to 30 minutes or till chicken is tender and no longer pink, brushing wings with the 3 sauces (8 wings per sauce) the last 5 minutes of cooking.

To Cook by Direct Grill Method: Grill chicken wings on the grill rack of an uncovered grill directly over *medium* coals about 20 minutes or till chicken is tender and no longer pink, turning occasionally and brushing wings with the 3 sauces (8 wings per sauce) the last 5 minutes of cooking.

To Serve: Transfer remaining sauces to separate serving bowls and use for dipping sauces.

Per serving: 482 calories / 28 g protein / 46 g carbohydrate / 19 g fat (5 g saturated) / 82 mg cholesterol / 1,174 mg sodium / 485 mg potassium.

Grilled Quesadillas

Grilled Quesadillas

Indirect or Direct Grilling

Serves 6

Quesadillas:	6 7-inch flour tortillas
	2 tablespoons cooking oil
	½ cup salsa
	1½ cups shredded Monterey Jack cheese with jalapeño peppers *or* shredded Monterey Jack cheese (6 ounces)
Accompaniments:	Dairy sour cream, guacamole, *and/or* salsa
	Cilantro sprigs (optional)

The pepper cheese makes these appetizer-size servings plenty hot. For a milder flavor, use the plain Monterey Jack cheese in the filling. Sour cream and/or guacamole and salsa add extra flavor.

For Quesadillas: Brush one side of 3 of the tortillas with some of the cooking oil. Place tortillas, oil side down, on a large baking sheet. Spread salsa over each tortilla on baking sheet. Sprinkle each with cheese. Top with remaining tortillas. Brush top tortillas with remaining oil.

To Cook by Indirect Grill Method: In a covered grill arrange preheated coals for indirect grilling. Test for *medium* heat where quesadillas will cook. Place quesadillas on the grill rack not over coals. Cover and grill about 4 to 5 minutes or till cheese begins to melt and tortillas start to brown, turning once.

To Cook by Direct Grill Method: Grill quesadillas on the grill rack of an uncovered grill directly over *medium* coals for 3 to 4 minutes or till cheese begins to melt and tortillas start to brown, turning once.

To Serve: Cut quesadillas into wedges. Top each with a dab of sour cream, guacamole, and/or salsa, and if desired, cilantro.

Per serving: 289 calories / 10 protein / 20 g carbohydrate / 19 g fat (9 g saturated) / 34 mg cholesterol / 236 mg sodium / 109 mg potassium.

Bacon-Wrapped Vegetables

Indirect or Direct Grilling   Serves 8

Kabobs:	12	slices bacon
	8	pearl onions
	1	small zucchini
	8	medium mushroom caps
Sauce:	2	tablespoons dry sherry
	2	tablespoons soy sauce
	1	teaspoon sugar
	¼	teaspoon garlic powder
	¼	teaspoon ground ginger

Each appetizer-size serving features a skewer with a bacon-wrapped pearl onion, a chunk of zucchini, and a mushroom cap.

To Prepare Kabobs: Cut bacon slices in half crosswise. In a large skillet cook bacon about 4 minutes or till partially cooked. Drain well on paper towels. In a small saucepan cook the onions, covered, in a small amount of boiling water for 4 minutes. Drain. Cut eight 1-inch-thick slices from the zucchini (reserve remaining zucchini for another use). Wrap 1 piece of bacon around each onion, each zucchini slice, and each mushroom cap.

On eight 6-inch skewers, alternately thread onions, zucchini, and mushrooms, leaving about ¼ inch between pieces.

For Sauce: In a small mixing bowl combine all sauce ingredients.

To Cook by Indirect Grill Method: In a covered grill arrange preheated coals around a drip pan. Test for *medium* heat above the pan. Place kabobs on the grill rack over the drip pan. Cover and grill for 8 to 10 minutes or till bacon is crisp and browned, turning once and brushing frequently with sauce.

To Cook by Direct Grill Method: Grill kabobs on the grill rack of an uncovered grill directly over *medium* coals for 8 to 10 minutes or till bacon is crisp and browned, turning once and brushing twice with brushing sauce.

Per serving: 75 calories / 4 g protein / 4 g carbohydrate / 5 g fat (2 g saturated) / 8 mg cholesterol / 410 mg sodium / 170 mg potassium.

MARINADES, SAUCES, & RELISHES

Want to add Oriental spice, Italian zest, or all-American

jazz to your grilled specialty? You can, with a

simply-spiced marinade, relish, or sauce from this

chapter. Make them, then forget them till grill-time.

They'll carry the show!

Red Wine and Peppercorn Marinade

Marinade:

⅔ cup dry red wine

½ cup cooking oil

2 tablespoons cracked whole
  black pepper

2 tablespoons snipped fresh thyme
  or 1 teaspoon dried thyme, crushed

2 bay leaves

¼ teaspoon salt

A great marinade for about 1 pound of meat, such as beef sirloin steak or beef cubes for kabobs.

For Marinade: In a small mixing bowl combine all ingredients. Place 1 to 2 pounds *beef steaks, cubes,* or *roast* in a plastic bag set into a deep bowl or shallow dish. Pour marinade over meat in bag. Seal bag and turn meat to coat well. Marinate in the refrigerator for 6 to 24 hours, turning bag occasionally. Remove meat from bag, reserving marinade if desired.

To Cook: Grill meat according to the charts on pages 230-232. If desired, cook meat for half the time specified and brush meat with marinade. Continue grilling for remaining time or till desired doneness; do not brush with marinade. Makes about 1¼ cups marinade (about 20 tablespoons).

Per tablespoon: 55 calories / 0 g protein / 0 g carbohydrate / 5 g fat (1 g saturated) / 0 mg cholesterol / 27 mg sodium / 13 mg potassium.

Lemon-Rosemary Marinade

Marinade:

1 teaspoon finely shredded lemon peel

⅓ cup lemon juice

¼ cup olive oil *or* cooking oil

¼ cup white wine Worcestershire sauce

1 tablespoon sugar

1 tablespoon snipped fresh rosemary,
  basil, *or* thyme *or* 1 teaspoon dried
  rosemary, basil, *or* thyme, crushed

¼ teaspoon salt

⅛ teaspoon pepper

Use this marinade for about 1½ pounds of fish, such as salmon, halibut, shark, swordfish, or tuna steaks.

For Marinade: In a small mixing bowl combine all ingredients. Place 1 to 1½ pounds *fish* in a plastic bag set into a shallow dish. Pour marinade over fish in bag. Seal bag and turn fish to coat well. Marinate in in the refrigerator for 1 to 2 hours, turning bag occasionally. Remove fish from bag, reserving marinade if desired.

To Cook: Grill fish according to the chart on page 233. If desired, cook fish for half the time specified and brush fish with the marinade. Continue grilling for remaining time or just till fish begins to flake; do not brush with marinade. Makes about ¾ cup marinade (about 12 tablespoons).

Per tablespoon: 49 calories / 0 g protein / 3 g carbohydrate / 5 g fat (1 g saturated) / 0 mg cholesterol / 87 mg sodium / 23 mg potassium.

Garlic and Basil Marinade

Marinade:	
⅔	cup dry white wine *or* white wine vinegar
⅓	cup olive *or* cooking oil
1	green onion, sliced (2 tablespoons)
2	tablespoons snipped fresh basil, oregano, *or* rosemary *or*
	1½ teaspoons dried basil, oregano, *or* rosemary, crushed
1	teaspoon sugar
2	cloves garlic, minced

Try this marinade with about 2 pounds of meaty chicken pieces, such as breasts, thighs, and drumsticks.

For Marinade: In a small mixing bowl combine all ingredients. Place 2 to 2½ pounds meaty *chicken pieces* in a plastic bag set into a deep bowl or shallow dish. Pour marinade over chicken in bag. Seal bag and turn chicken to coat well. Marinate in the refrigerator for 6 to 24 hours, turning bag occasionally. Remove chicken from bag, reserving marinade if desired.

To Cook: Grill chicken according to the charts on pages 228-229. If desired, cook chicken for half the time specified and brush chicken with the marinade. Continue grilling for remaining time or till chicken is tender and no longer pink; do not brush with marinade. Makes about 1 cup marinade (about 16 tablespoons).

Per tablespoon: 48 calories / 0 g protein / 0 g carbohydrate / 5 g fat (1 g saturated) / 0 mg cholesterol / 1 mg sodium / 12 mg potassium.

Sweet 'n' Zesty Brush-On Sauce

Sauce:	
1	12-ounce can (1½ cups) unsweetened pineapple juice
¾	cup catsup
⅓	cup packed brown sugar
⅓	cup cider vinegar
1	tablespoon soy sauce
1	teaspoon prepared mustard
⅛	teaspoon salt
½	cup chopped pimiento-stuffed olives

Pimiento-stuffed olives and pineapple juice are the unique ingredients in this sauce that's brushed on the last 10 minutes of grilling.

For Sauce: In a medium saucepan combine pineapple juice, catsup, brown sugar, vinegar, soy sauce, mustard, and salt. Bring to boiling; reduce heat. Boil gently, uncovered, for 30 to 35 minutes or till desired consistency, stirring occasionally. Remove from heat. Stir in olives. Brush over *hamburgers*, *chicken*, or *meat and vegetable kabobs* the last 10 minutes of grilling. Pass any remaining sauce. Makes about 1¾ cups sauce (about 28 tablespoons).

Per tablespoon: 27 calories / 0 g protein / 6 g carbohydrate / 0 g fat (0 g saturated) / 0 mg cholesterol / 172 mg sodium / 63 mg potassium.

Plum-Good Barbecue Sauce

Shiitake Mushroom and
Shallot Sauce

Plum-Good Barbecue Sauce

Sauce:

1	medium onion, chopped (½ cup)
1	tablespoon margarine *or* butter
1	17-ounce can whole, unpitted purple plums
1	6-ounce can frozen lemonade concentrate, thawed
¼	cup catsup
2	tablespoons soy sauce
2	teaspoons prepared mustard
1	teaspoon ground ginger
1	teaspoon Worcestershire sauce

Just like the name says— this sauce is based on a can of purple plums. It's a good choice to use on poultry.

For Sauce: In a medium saucepan cook onion in margarine or butter till tender but not brown. Drain plums, reserving syrup.

Remove pits from plums; discard pits. In a blender container or food processor bowl combine plums and reserved syrup. Cover and blend or process till smooth. Stir plum puree, lemonade concentrate, catsup, soy sauce, mustard, ginger, and Worcestershire sauce into the onion mixture. Bring to boiling; reduce heat. Simmer, uncovered, for 10 to 15 minutes or till desired consistency, stirring occasionally. Brush over *chicken* or *ribs* the last 10 minutes of grilling. Pass any remaining sauce. Makes about 3 cups sauce (48 tablespoons).

Per tablespoon: 21 calories / 0 g protein / 5 g carbohydrate / 0 g fat (0 g saturated) / 0 mg cholesterol / 66 mg sodium / 23 mg potassium.

Shiitake Mushroom and Shallot Sauce

Sauce:

¾	cup sliced shiitake mushrooms
2	tablespoons finely chopped shallot *or* onion
1	tablespoon margarine *or* butter
1	tablespoon all-purpose flour
⅛	teaspoon salt
	Dash pepper
⅔	cup milk
½	cup dairy sour cream
1	tablespoon snipped parsley

For Sauce: In a small saucepan cook the mushrooms and shallot or onion in the margarine or butter. Stir in flour, salt, and pepper. Add milk all at once. Cook and stir till thickened and bubbly. Cook and stir for 2 minutes more. Stir in sour cream and parsley. Serve immediately with *beef* or *pork*. Makes about 1⅓ cups sauce (about 21 tablespoons).

Plan to serve about 3 tablespoons of this mixture with each portion of meat or fish. If you have any sauce leftover, cover and store it overnight in the refrigerator; reheat the sauce over low heat the next day.

Per tablespoon: 24 calories / 1 g protein / 2 g carbohydrate / 2 g fat (1 g saturated) / 3 mg cholesterol / 26 mg sodium / 29 mg potassium.

Basic Barbecue Sauce

Sauce:

¼ cup finely chopped onion
¼ cup finely chopped celery
1 tablespoon margarine *or* butter
¾ cup water
¾ cup catsup
¼ cup lemon juice
2 tablespoons brown sugar
2 tablespoons Worcestershire sauce
½ teaspoon dry mustard

Keep this all-purpose sauce in mind to brush on a variety of meats and chicken.

For Sauce: In a medium saucepan cook onion and celery in margarine or butter till tender but not brown. Stir in remaining ingredients. Bring to boiling; reduce heat. Simmer, uncovered, for 30 to 40 minutes or till reduced to 1¼ cups, stirring occasionally. Brush over *meat* or *poultry* the last 10 minutes of grilling. Pass any remaining sauce. Makes about 1¼ cups sauce (20 tablespoons).

Per tablespoon: 23 calories / 0 g protein / 5 g carbohydrate / 1 g fat (0 g saturated) / 0 mg cholesterol / 130 mg sodium / 72 mg potassium.

Chili-Beer Sauce

Sauce:

1½ cups chili sauce
½ of a 12-ounce can (¾ cup) beer
1 small onion, finely chopped (⅓ cup)
2 tablespoons vinegar
1 tablespoon Worcestershire sauce
2 teaspoons brown sugar
   Several drops bottled hot pepper sauce

This sauce may be stored, covered, in the refrigerator for up to 1 week.

For Sauce: In a medium saucepan combine all ingredients. Bring to boiling; reduce heat. Simmer, uncovered, for 10 to 15 minutes or till desired consistency, stirring occasionally. Brush over *meat* or *poultry* the last 10 minutes of grilling. Pass any remaining sauce. Makes about 2 cups sauce (about 32 tablespoons).

Per tablespoon: 16 calories / 0 g protein / 4 g carbohydrate / 0 g fat (0 g saturated) / 0 mg cholesterol / 156 mg sodium / 52 mg potassium.

Basil-Cream Sauce

Sauce:	2 green onions, sliced (¼ cup)
	2 tablespoons margarine *or* butter
	½ cup whipping cream
	4 teaspoons snipped fresh basil *or* 1 teaspoon dried basil, crushed
	¼ teaspoon coarsely cracked black pepper
	1 tablespoon grated Parmesan cheese

The whipping cream and margarine make this a rich sauce to spoon over servings of grilled chicken or beef.

For Sauce: In a small saucepan cook green onions in margarine or butter till tender. Stir in whipping cream, basil, and pepper. Bring to boiling. Boil for 4 to 5 minutes or till slightly thickened, stirring occasionally. Remove saucepan from heat. Stir in Parmesan cheese. Serve with grilled *chicken* or *beef*. Makes about ½ cup sauce (about 8 tablespoons).

Per tablespoon: 81 calories / 1 g protein / 1 g carbohydrate / 9 g fat (4 g saturated) / 21 mg cholesterol / 54 mg sodium / 20 mg potassium.

Mushroom-Butter Sauce

Sauce:	½ cup butter *or* margarine
	2 cups sliced fresh mushrooms
	1 clove garlic, minced
	1 tablespoon snipped fresh oregano *or* 1 teaspoon dried oregano, crushed
	Dash pepper
	1 teaspoon finely shredded lemon peel

Lemon peel adds a wonderful tang to the mushrooms sauteed in butter. Spoon the mixture over grilled steak, chicken, or fish.

For Sauce: In a medium saucepan melt butter or margarine. Add mushrooms, garlic, oregano, and pepper. Cook about 5 minutes or till mushrooms are tender. Stir in lemon peel. Serve with grilled *steak*, *poultry*, or *fish*. Makes about 1 cup sauce (about 16 tablespoons).

Per tablespoon: 53 calories / 0 g protein / 1 g carbohydrate / 6 g fat (4 g saturated) / 15 mg cholesterol / 58 mg sodium / 36 mg potassium.

Ginger-Garlic Sauce

Sauce:	
	2 green onions, sliced (¼ cup)
	½ teaspoon grated gingerroot
	1 clove garlic, minced
	1 tablespoon cooking oil *or* olive oil
	½ cup cold water
	1½ teaspoons cornstarch
	1 teaspoon soy sauce
	1 teaspoon oyster sauce (optional)

Try the sauce over grilled shrimp, chicken, steak, or pork chops.

For Sauce: In a small saucepan cook and stir green onions, gingerroot, and garlic in hot oil for 1 minute. In a small mixing bowl stir together water, cornstarch, and soy sauce. Add to onion mixture in the saucepan. Cook and stir over medium heat till mixture is thickened and bubbly. Cook and stir for 2 minutes more. If desired, stir in oyster sauce. Remove from heat. Serve hot with grilled *shrimp, chicken, steak,* or *pork chops.* Makes about ⅔ cup sauce (about 11 tablespoons).

Per tablespoon: 13 calories / 0 g protein / 1 g carbohydrate / 1 g fat (0 g saturated) / 0 mg cholesterol / 32 mg sodium / 5 mg potassium.

Cucumber-Yogurt Sauce with Mint

Sauce:	
	⅓ cup plain yogurt
	¼ cup chopped, seeded cucumber
	¼ cup finely chopped carrot
	3 tablespoons mayonnaise *or* salad dressing
	1 teaspoon snipped fresh mint *or* ¼ teaspoon dried mint, crushed

Contrast the piping hot temperature of grilled chicken or fish with this chilled sauce.

For Sauce: In a small mixing bowl combine all ingredients. Cover and chill for 2 to 24 hours. Serve with grilled *chicken* or *fish.*

Makes about ¾ cup sauce (about 12 tablespoons).

Per tablespoon: 30 calories / 0 g protein / 1 g carbohydrate / 3 g fat (0 g saturated) / 2 mg cholesterol / 25 mg sodium / 27 mg potassium.

Honey-Mustard Brush-On Sauce

Sauce:	⅓ cup honey
	3 tablespoons Dijon-style mustard
	2 tablespoons finely chopped onion
	2 tablespoons apple cider *or* apple juice
	⅛ teaspoon ground red pepper

Red pepper and Dijon-style mustard give this honey-of-a-sauce a pleasant hotness and flavor.

For Sauce: In a small saucepan combine all ingredients. Bring to boiling; reduce heat. Boil gently, uncovered, for 5 to 7 minutes or till onion is tender and sauce is slightly thickened. Brush over *meat* or *poultry* the last 10 minutes of grilling. Pass any remaining sauce. Makes about ½ cup sauce (about 8 tablespoons).

Per tablespoon: 53 calories / 0 g protein / 12 g carbohydrate / 0 g fat (0 g saturated) / 0 mg cholesterol / 135 mg sodium / 25 mg potassium.

Easy Glaze

Glaze:	⅓ cup orange marmalade *or* apricot preserves
	⅓ cup bottled barbecue sauce
	1 teaspoon white wine Worcestershire sauce

You'll only need 3 ingredients to make this simple rib or chicken brush-on.

For Glaze: In a small mixing bowl combine marmalade or preserves, barbecue sauce, and Worcestershire sauce. Brush over *ribs* or *chicken* the last 10 to 15 minutes of grilling. Makes about ⅔ cup sauce (about 11 tablespoons).

Per tablespoon: 33 calories / 0 g protein / 8 g carbohydrate / 0 g fat (0 g saturated) / 0 mg cholesterol / 66 mg sodium / 23 mg potassium.

Tomato-
Apple Chutney

Italian Squash
Relish

Tomato-Apple Chutney

Chutney:		
	3	medium tomatoes (about 1 pound), chopped
	2	medium cooking apples (about 12 ounces), cored and chopped
	½	cup sugar
	⅓	cup vinegar
	¼	cup chopped green pepper
	¼	cup raisins
	¼	cup water
	1	tablespoon lime or lemon juice
	1	teaspoon ground cinnamon
	2	cloves garlic, minced
	¼	teaspoon salt

Serve it warm or serve it cold. Either way, the chutney adds a pleasant flavor, and few calories, to grilled meat or poultry.

For Chutney: In a large saucepan combine all ingredients. Bring to boiling; reduce heat. Cover and simmer for 30 minutes, stirring occasionally. Uncover and cook for 15 minutes. Cool to room temperature. To store, cover and chill in the refrigerator up to 1 week. Serve with grilled *meat* or *poultry*. Makes about 3 cups chutney (about 48 tablespoons).

Per tablespoon: 15 calories / 0 g protein / 4 g carbohydrate / 0 g fat (0 g saturated) / 0 mg cholesterol / 12 mg sodium / 33 mg potassium.

Italian Squash Relish

Relish:		
	1	medium onion, chopped (½ cup)
	1	clove garlic, minced
	2	tablespoons olive oil or cooking oil
	2	medium zucchini or yellow summer squash, chopped (2 cups)
	1	8-ounce can stewed tomatoes
	1	8-ounce can pizza sauce
	¼	teaspoon dried oregano, crushed
	¼	teaspoon dried rosemary, crushed
	¼	teaspoon dried thyme, crushed
		Dash salt
		Dash pepper

A sensational way to use zucchini or other fresh summer squash.

For Relish: In a medium saucepan cook onion and garlic in hot oil till onion is tender but not brown. Stir in the zucchini or summer squash, *undrained* tomatoes, pizza sauce, oregano, rosemary, thyme, salt, and pepper. Bring the mixture to boiling; reduce heat. Cover and simmer about 10 minutes or till vegetables are tender. Uncover and simmer about 20 minutes more or till relish is desired consistency. Serve relish hot or cold over grilled *chicken* or *meat*. To store, cover and chill in the refrigerator for up to 1 week. Makes about 2½ cups relish (about 40 tablespoons).

Per tablespoon: 13 calories / 0 g protein / 1 g carbohydrate / 1 g fat (0 g saturated) / 0 mg cholesterol / 61 mg sodium / 57 mg potassium.

Gazpacho Sauce

Sauce:

1	medium tomato, seeded and finely chopped
¼	cup chopped, seeded cucumber
2	tablespoon chopped green pepper
1	green onion, thinly sliced (2 tablespoons)
1	tablespoon red wine vinegar
1	tablespoon olive oil *or* cooking oil
½	teaspoon sugar
⅛	teaspoon garlic salt
	Dash pepper

This sauce is reminiscent of the chilled tomato soup that has its roots in Spanish cooking. Allow about ¼ cup per serving.

For Sauce: In a small mixing bowl stir together all ingredients. Cover and chill for 2 to 24 hours, stirring occasionally. Serve with a slotted spoon and pass with grilled *chicken* or *fish*. Makes about 1 cup sauce (about 16 tablespoons).

Per tablespoon: 10 calories / 0 g protein / 1 g carbohydrate / 1 g fat (0 g saturated) / 0 mg cholesterol / 14 mg sodium / 22 mg potassium.

Apricot-Grape Salsa

Salsa:

1	tablespoon honey
1	teaspoon cornstarch
⅛	teaspoon ground nutmeg
	Dash ground ginger
½	cup chopped pitted apricots *or* peaches
¼	cup finely chopped celery
3	tablespoons orange juice
1	teaspoon lemon juice
1	teaspoon snipped fresh mint *or*
	¼ teaspoon dried mint, crushed
½	cup quartered seedless red grapes

Combine fruit, spices, and mint for an interest—and delicious—poultry accompaniment.

For Salsa: In a small saucepan stir together honey, cornstarch, nutmeg, and ginger. Stir in apricots, celery, orange juice, lemon juice, and mint. Cook and stir till thickened and bubbly. Cook and stir for 2 minutes more. Stir in grapes. Pour into a small bowl. Cover and chill till serving time. Serve with grilled *chicken* or *turkey*. Makes about 1 cup salsa (14 tablespoons).

Per tablespoon: 15 calories / 0 g protein / 4 g carbohydrate / 0 g fat (0 g saturated) / 0 mg cholesterol / 4 mg sodium / 50 mg potassium.

STAY-AT-HOME-AND-PARTY MENUS

So you're dining in—what better way to feed your family and friends than with our thoughtfully assembled menus? Appealing meal plans for groups of 4, 6, 8, and 12 are woven throughout this chapter. Peruse them, then use them as you choose. Bon appétit!

Fun Family Barbecue for 4

■

Give your family a barbecue dinner any night of the week. Grill the hearty summer foods they all love: burgers, corn, and potatoes. With this simple menu, you can dig in just 60 minutes after lighting the coals.

■

Giant Stuffed Burger with Texas Toast*

■

Cheese and Peas Potatoes*

■

Corn on the cob

■

Strawberries and peaches topped with fresh whipped cream

*Recipes on pages 208-209.

Giant Stuffed Burger with Texas Toast

Indirect or Direct Grilling   Serves 4

Meat Mixture:	1 beaten egg
	¼ cup quick-cooking rolled oats
	2 tablespoons bottled barbecue sauce
	¼ teaspoon salt
	⅛ teaspoon pepper
	1 pound ground beef, pork, *or* lamb
Stuffing:	¼ cup coarsely shredded carrot
	¼ cup finely chopped celery
	2 green onions, thinly sliced (¼ cup)
	1 2-ounce can mushroom stems and pieces, drained
Topping:	Bottled barbecue sauce
Bread:	4 slices Texas toast, toasted and halved diagonally

Serve the burger with all your favorite accompaniments, such as pickle slices or relish, lettuce leaves, tomato slices, mustard, and catsup.

To Prepare Meat Mixture: In a medium bowl stir together egg, oats, barbecue sauce, salt, and pepper. Add meat; mix well. Divide mixture in half. On waxed paper, pat *each* half into a 7-inch circle.

For Stuffing: In a small mixing bowl combine all stuffing ingredients. Spoon over *one* circle of meat to within 1 inch of the edge. Top with second circle of meat; peel off top sheet of waxed paper and seal edges of meat together.

To Cook by Indirect Grill Method: In a covered grill arrange preheated coals around a drip pan. Test for *medium* heat above the pan. Carefully invert the meat patty onto the grill rack over the drip pan; peel off remaining waxed paper. Cover and grill for 35 to 45 minutes or till no pink remains.

To Cook by Direct Grill Method: Invert meat patty onto a well-greased wire grill basket; peel off remaining waxed paper. Grill on the grill rack of an uncovered grill directly over *medium* coals about 22 minutes or till no pink remains, turning once halfway through grilling time.

To Serve: Brush burger with additional barbecue sauce. Cut into wedges and serve with Texas toast.

Per serving: 339 calories / 27 g protein / 25 g carbohydrate / 14 g fat (5 g saturated) / 125 mg cholesterol / 581 mg sodium / 354 mg potassium.

Cheese and Peas Potatoes

Direct Grilling   Serves 4

Vegetables:	1 4-ounce container cheese spread with mild Mexican flavor (½ cup)
	½ of a 16-ounce package (2 cups) loose-pack frozen hash brown potatoes with onion and peppers
	¾ cup loose-pack frozen peas
	¼ cup chopped salami

This hearty, family-style side dish is an easy, cheesy, vegetable mixture for four.

To Prepare Vegetables: Spoon cheese spread into a medium saucepan; cook and stir over low heat till melted. Stir potatoes, peas, and salami into cheese.

To Prepare Packet: Tear off two 22x18-inch pieces of heavy foil. Make a double thickness of foil that measures 22x18. Place the potato mixture in center of the foil. Bring up two opposite edges of foil and seal with a double fold. Then fold remaining ends to completely enclose the potato mixture, leaving space for steam to build.

To Cook by Direct Grill Method: Grill foil packet on the grill rack of a grill directly over *medium* to *medium-high* coals for 17 to 25 minutes or till heated through, turning frequently.

Per serving: 201 calories / 9 g protein / 20 g carbohydrate / 10 g fat (5 g saturated) / 23 mg cholesterol / 617 mg sodium / 363 mg potassium.

SMOKED TURKEY
DINNER FOR 6

■

*Come the weekend, you want to relax with
your family and friends. This leisurely menu lets
you do just that— the turkey smokes
unattended in a covered grill.*

■

Raclette-Style Cheese*

■

Smoked Turkey with
Orange Glaze*

■

Honey Mustard Slaw*

■

Iced Lime Tea* or Peachy
Lemonade*

■

Fudge brownies with vanilla
ice cream

*Recipes on pages 212-215.

Raclette-Style Cheese

Direct Grilling   Serves 6

Cheese Mixture:	1½	cups shredded process Gruyère *or* process Swiss cheese (6 ounces)
	1	cup shredded Gouda cheese (4 ounces)
	1	tablespoon snipped fresh basil *or* oregano *or* 1 teaspoon dried basil *or* oregano, crushed
	2	teaspoons Dijon-style mustard
	1	teaspoon white wine Worcestershire sauce
		Several dashes bottled hot pepper sauce
Garnish:		Pimiento slices (optional)
		Fresh thyme, rosemary, *and/or* savory sprigs (optional)
Accompaniment:		Blanched cauliflower *and/or* broccoli flowerets, boiled halved tiny new potatoes, *and/or* pita bread wedges*

It's important to use process Gruyère or Swiss cheese rather than natural cheese. Process cheese melts smoothly, giving a velvety texture.

The nutrition information for this appetizer was calculated using ¼ cup vegetables and 2 pita bread wedges.

For Cheese Mixture: In a small mixer bowl or food processor bowl combine cheeses; let stand to soften. Add basil or oregano, mustard, Worcestershire sauce, and hot pepper sauce; beat with an electric mixer on low speed or cover and process till well combined. (Mixture will be crumbly.) Form into a ball. Shape into a 4½-inch round, about 1 inch high. Wrap in clear plastic wrap; chill several hours or overnight.

To Cook by Direct Grill Method: Unwrap cheese round; place in a 6-inch cast-iron skillet or heavy pan. Cut into 6 wedges; separate wedges slightly. Place skillet or pan on the grill rack of grill. Grill directly over *low* coals. Cover and grill for 5 to 7 minutes or till softened and heated through, checking often to make sure the cheese doesn't overmelt. (The cheese shouldn't lose its shape or start to run.)

To Serve: If desired, top each wedge of cheese with a pimiento slice and a herb sprig. Serve with warm vegetables and/or bread.

*Note: To blanch cauliflower and broccoli flowerets, cook in boiling water, uncovered, for 2 minutes. Drain. For tiny new potatoes, cook in boiling water, covered, for 10 to 15 minutes or till tender. Drain.

If you like, blanch or boil the vegetables ahead of time; cover and chill. Wrap vegetables in foil and reheat them on the grill while the cheese is heating. *Or*, place vegetables in a microwave-safe dish and reheat in the microwave oven.

Per serving: 219 calories / 15 g protein / 7 g carbohydrate / 15 g fat (9 g saturated) / 52 mg cholesterol / 355 mg sodium / 144 mg potassium.

Smoked Turkey with Orange Glaze

Indirect Grilling   Serves 6

Glaze:	1	10-ounce jar orange marmalade (about 1 cup)
	2	tablespoons lemon juice
	1	teaspoon prepared mustard
		Dash ground cloves
Wood Chips:	4	cups mesquite chips
Poultry:	1	3- to 3½-pound bone-in turkey breast half
Accompaniment:		Orange slices, halved (optional)

Make sure that the drip pan is large enough to cover the area under the turkey breast half so that all the drippings fall into the pan.

For Glaze: In a small saucepan cook and stir all glaze ingredients over low heat till melted. Set glaze aside.

To Prepare Wood Chips: About 1 hour before grilling, soak mesquite chips in enough water to cover. Drain the chips before using.

To Cook by Indirect Grill Method: In a covered grill arrange preheated coals around a drip pan. Pour 1 inch of water into the drip pan. Sprinkle *half* of the drained wood chips onto the preheated coals. Test for *medium* heat above the pan. Insert meat thermometer into thickest part of turkey, making sure bulb does not touch bone. Place turkey on the grill rack over the drip pan. Cover and grill for 45 minutes. Add drained chips and more briquettes. Cover and grill for ¾ to 1¼ hours more or till meat thermometer registers 170°, adding briquettes every 45 minutes. Brush with glaze. Cover and grill 5 minutes. Brush again with glaze. Cover and grill 5 minutes more. Cover and let stand 10 to 15 minutes before serving. If desired, serve with orange slices. Pass remaining glaze.

Per serving: 262 calories / 19 g protein / 34 g carbohydrate / 5 g fat (1 g saturated) / 51 mg cholesterol / 61 mg sodium / 245 mg potassium.

Honey Mustard Slaw

Serves 6

Dressing:	½ cup mayonnaise *or* salad dressing
	½ cup dairy sour cream
	2 tablespoons honey
	1 to 2 tablespoons Dijon-style *or* coarse-grain brown mustard
Vegetables:	3 cups coarsely shredded cabbage (about ½ of a medium head)*
	2 cups coarsely shredded romaine*
	1 small jicama, peeled and shredded (2 cups)
	2 green onions, sliced (¼ cup)
Nuts:	½ cup toasted broken pecans

*Short on time?
Then substitute 3 cups of
preshredded cabbage instead
of shredding your own.
You'll find the preshredded
variety in the produce
section of your supermarket.*

For Dressing: In a small mixing bowl stir together all dressing ingredients. Cover and chill.

For Vegetables: In a large salad bowl combine cabbage, romaine, jicama, and green onions; cover and chill.

To Serve: Add dressing to cabbage mixture; toss to coat. Sprinkle with pecans.

Note: To coarsely shred cabbage, hold a quarter-head of cabbage firmly against the cutting board. Use a chef's knife to slice the cabbage into long, coarse shreds. To coarsely shred romaine, stack the leaves and use a chef's knife to slice crosswise into long, coarse shreds.

Per serving: 292 calories / 3 g protein / 16 g carbohydrate / 25 g fat (5 g saturated) / 19 mg cholesterol / 182 mg sodium / 221 mg potassium.

Iced Lime Tea

Tea:	5	cups cold strong tea
	1	6-ounce can (¾ cup) frozen limeade concentrate, thawed
		Ice cubes
		Sake (optional)
Garnish:		Halved lime slices (optional)

To make the strong tea for this smooth, sweet-tart drink, our Test Kitchen brewed 6 tea bags in 5 cups boiling water.

For Tea: In a pitcher combine the cold tea and the limeade concentrate.

To Serve: Pour tea mixture into individual ice-filled glasses. If desired, add *2 tablespoons* sake to each serving and garnish with lime slices. Make 6 servings.

Per serving: 55 calories / 0 g protein / 15 g carbohydrate / 0 g fat (0 g saturated) / 0 mg cholesterol / 6 mg sodium / 90 mg potassium.

Peachy Lemonade

Lemonade:	3	cups cold water
	1	cup lemon juice
	¾	cup sugar
		Ice cubes
	1	29-ounce can peach slices, chilled
Garnish:		Peach *or* nectarine slices (optional)

Save your guests a few calories by substituting juice-pack peaches for the syrup-pack kind.

For Lemonade: In a pitcher stir together the water, lemon juice, and sugar till sugar is dissolved. Place *half* of the *undrained* peach slices in a blender container with *half* of the lemonade mixture. Cover; blend till smooth. Repeat with remaining peaches and lemonade. Stir all together in the pitcher. If desired, chill the lemonade.

To Serve: Pour into individual ice-filled glasses. If desired, garnish with peach or nectarine slices. Makes 6 servings.

Per serving: 182 calories / 1 g protein / 50 g carbohydrate / 0 g fat (0 g saturated) / 0 mg cholesterol / 13 mg sodium / 198 mg potassium.

BACKYARD
COOKOUT FOR 8

■

*Next time you get the urge to barbecue, invite
some folks over for this sumptuous feast. It's easy
to serve these recipes—you put most of them
together ahead so they're ready to grill. While
they sizzle, you're free to join in yard games.*

■

Caramelized Onion and
Cheese Bites*

■

Salmon Roast with
Marinated Vegetables*

■

Spinach Couscous Salad*

■

Nectarine Sunrise*

■

Fresh fruit with pineapple sorbet

*Recipes on pages 218-221.

Caramelized Onion and Cheese Bites

Direct Grilling   Serves 8

Seasoning:	1	large onion, halved and thinly sliced
	1	tablespoon olive oil *or* cooking oil
	⅓	cup coarsely chopped walnuts
	1	teaspoon sugar
	1	tablespoon herb mustard *or* Dijon-style mustard
Bread:	16	¼-inch-thick slices baguette French bread *or* other long, thin firm bread
	½	cup freshly grated Parmesan *or* Romano cheese

Cook these sweet, golden nibbles alongside the salmon on the grill.

For Seasoning: In a large skillet cook the sliced onion in hot oil about 3 minutes or just till tender. Add the walnuts and the sugar. Continue to cook and stir about 5 minutes more or till the onion is slightly caramelized and walnuts are lightly toasted. Stir in the mustard.

For Bread: Spoon some of the onion mixture on each of the bread slices. Sprinkle with the cheese. If desired, cover bread slices and let stand at room temperature up to 1 hour.

To Cook by Direct Grill Method: Grill bread slices, onion side up, on the grill rack of a grill directly over *medium-high* coals about 2 minutes or just till bottoms are toasted and slices are heated through. Watch bread slices carefully the last 30 seconds to avoid overbrowning.

Per serving: 205 calories / 8 g protein / 25 g carbohydrate / 8 g fat (1 g saturated) / 5 mg cholesterol / 360 mg sodium / 96 mg potassium.

Salmon Roast with Marinated Vegetables

Indirect Grilling	Marinating Time: 6 to 24 hours	Serves 8

Marinade:	⅓ cup dry white wine
	¼ cup cooking oil
	1 tablespoon white wine Worcestershire sauce
	1 tablespoon snipped fresh sage *or* 1 teaspoon dried sage, crushed
	½ teaspoon salt
	¼ teaspoon cracked black pepper
Vegetables:	1 medium red sweet pepper
	1 medium yellow sweet pepper
	1 medium zucchini
	6 green onions
Fish:	1 4-pound salmon roast (about 8 inches long and 2¼ inches thick), boned,
	or one 5- to 6-pound whole dressed salmon

You may need to special order the salmon roast from your fish market. It's a thick, center-cut portion from a large fish. Have the store bone it for you, too, if you like.

For Marinade: In a medium mixing bowl combine all marinade ingredients.

To Prepare Vegetables: Cut peppers and zucchini into thin 2-inch-long strips. Cut green onions into 2-inch pieces; sliver the pieces. Add vegetables to the marinade. Cover and chill 6 hours or overnight.

To Prepare Fish: Tear off a piece of heavy foil larger than the fish. Shape the foil into a pan; grease or spray foil with nonstick spray coating. Drain vegetable mixture, reserving marinade. Place fish in foil pan. Spoon as much of the pepper mixture as you can into the fish cavity. Set the remaining vegetable mixture aside. Brush fish lightly with the reserved marinade.

To Cook by Indirect Grill Method: In a covered grill arrange preheated coals for indirect grilling. Test for *medium* heat where the fish will cook. Place fish in foil pan on the grill rack not over the coals. Cover and grill for 40 minutes. Add any remaining vegetable mixture to the pan; brush fish with reserved marinade. Cover and grill 10 to 20 minutes longer or just till fish flakes with a fork.

Per serving: 283 calories / 33 g protein / 2 g carbohydrate / 15 g fat (3 g saturated) / 41 mg cholesterol / 1,536 mg sodium / 404 mg potassium.

Spinach Couscous Salad

Serves 8

Couscous:	1	cup chicken broth
	¾	cup couscous
	½	cup golden Caesar *or* Italian salad dressing
Salad:	2	cups shredded fresh spinach
	12	cherry tomatoes, halved
	½	of an 8-ounce can (½ cup) sliced water chestnuts, drained
		Spinach leaves

Look for couscous in the rice or pasta section of the supermarket. It's a grain product made from ground semolina and it has the shape of very tiny beads.

For Couscous: In a saucepan bring chicken broth to boiling; stir in couscous. Remove from heat. Cover and let stand for 5 minutes. Transfer to a bowl; add salad dressing. Cover and refrigerate for 2 to 4 hours or till couscous is completely chilled.

For Salad: Toss couscous mixture with shredded spinach, tomatoes, and water chestnuts. Serve on spinach leaves.

Per serving: 153 calories / 4 g protein / 17 g carbohydrate / 7 g fat (0 g saturated) / 0 mg cholesterol / 123 mg sodium / 255 mg potassium.

Nectarine Sunrise

Serves 8

Fruit:	4 nectarines
Beverage:	1 6-ounce can frozen orange juice concentrate, thawed
	⅔ cup tequila
	Crushed ice
	½ cup grenadine syrup
Garnish:	Fresh mint sprigs

To create the swirled red and gold effect shown on pages 216-217, use a swizzle stick or straw to stir the drink very lightly in a circular motion after pouring the nectarine mixture over the grenadine.

To Prepare Fruit Mixture: Pit and slice *one* of the nectarines; set aside for garnish. Halve, pit, and coarsely chop remaining nectarines.

For Beverage: In a blender container combine chopped nectarines, orange juice concentrate, and tequila; cover and blend till smooth. Gradually add crushed ice, blending till slushy and mixture measures *5 cups*.

To Serve: Place *1 tablespoon* of the grenadine syrup in *each* of 8 stemmed glasses. Add nectarine mixture. To garnish, top each with a mint sprig; hang a nectarine slice on the side of each glass. Serve at once. Makes 8 (5-ounce) servings.

Per serving: 142 calories / 1 g protein / 24 g carbohydrate / 0 g fat (0 g saturated) / 0 mg cholesterol / 17 mg sodium / 288 mg potassium.

SUPER SIZZLING MEAL FOR 12

■

A crisp, fall day is a perfect time to enjoy the robust flavors featured in this menu.

■

Marinated Pork Roast*

■

Walnut-Mushroom Salad*

■

Mustard-Sage French Bread*

■

Nutty Mocha Chip Ice Cream*

■

Mineral water or iced tea

*Recipes on pages 224-227.

Marinated Pork Roast

	Indirect Grilling	Marinating Time: 12 to 24 hours	Serves 12 to 16
Marinade:	1 cup apple juice		
	½ teaspoon dried sage, crushed		
	½ teaspoon salt		
	¼ teaspoon pepper		
	2 cloves garlic, minced		
Meat:	1 4-pound boneless pork top loin roast (double loin, tied)		

There's not much work involved with this main dish. Just marinate the piece of meat and grill till the temperature reaches 160° (for medium-well) to 170° (for well-done).

For Marinade: In a small mixing bowl combine all marinade ingredients.

To Prepare Meat: Trim fat from meat. Place meat in a plastic bag set into a deep bowl. Pour marinade over meat in bag. Seal bag and turn meat to coat well. Marinate in the refrigerator for 12 to 24 hours, turning bag occasionally. Remove meat from bag, reserving marinade.

To Cook by Indirect Grill Method: In a covered grill arrange preheated coals around a drip pan. Test for *medium-low* heat above the pan. Place meat on the grill rack over the drip pan. Cover and grill for 1½ to 2 hours, or till meat thermometer registers 160° or 170°, brushing meat occasionally with reserved marinade during first hour of cooking. Remove strings and slice meat to serve.

Per serving: 181 calories / 21 g protein / 0 g carbohydrate / 10 g fat (3 g saturated) / 68 mg cholesterol / 58 mg sodium / 273 mg potassium.

Walnut-Mushroom Salad

Serves 12

Vinaigrette:	3	tablespoons red wine vinegar *or* vinegar
	2	tablespoons walnut oil
	2	tablespoons salad oil
	2	teaspoons sugar
	1	teaspoon finely shredded lemon peel
	½	teaspoon salt
	⅛	teaspoon pepper
Salad:	10	cups torn mixed salad greens
	2	cups sliced fresh mushrooms
	2	medium apples, cored and chopped
	½	cup toasted broken walnuts

Select red apples for the salad and don't peel them. The red adds a spark of color to this tossed salad.

For Vinagrette: In a screw-top jar combine all vinaigrette ingredients. Cover and shake well. Store in the refrigerator for up to 2 weeks. Shake well before using.

To Prepare Salad: In a large salad bowl combine greens, mushrooms, apples, and walnuts. Shake vinaigrette well; pour over lettuce mixture. Toss lightly to coat.

Per serving: 99 calories / 2 g protein / 7 g carbohydrate / 8 g fat (1 g saturated) / 0 mg cholesterol / 110 mg sodium / 265 mg potassium.

Mustard-Sage French Bread

Direct Grilling   Serves 12

Spread:	¼ cup margarine *or* butter, softened
	1 tablespoon snipped fresh sage *or* ¼ teaspoon dried sage, crushed
	1 to 2 teaspoons Dijon-style *or* prepared mustard
Bread:	1 16-ounce loaf unsliced French bread

Heat the bread on the grill next to the meat the last 15 minutes of cooking.

For Spread: In a small mixing bowl stir together all spread ingredients.

For Bread: Cut the bread into 24 slices, *cutting to but not through* bottom crust. Spread cut surfaces with spread. Tear off a 48x18-inch piece of heavy foil. Fold in half to make a double thickness of foil that measures 24x18 inches. Place bread in the center of the foil. Bring up two opposite edges of foil and seal with a double fold. Then fold remaining ends to completely enclose the bread, leaving space for steam to build.

To Cook by Direct Grill Method: Grill bread on the grill rack of a grill directly over *medium* coals about 15 minutes or till bread is heated through.

Per serving: 140 calories / 4 g protein / 19 g carbohydrate / 5 g fat (1 g saturated) / 0 mg cholesterol / 263 mg sodium / 35 mg potassium.

Nutty Mocha Chip Ice Cream

Serves 12

Nuts:	1 cup chopped pecans
	1 tablespoon margarine *or* butter
Ice Cream:	2 squares (2 ounces) unsweetened chocolate
	1½ cups sugar
	1 envelope unflavored gelatin
	4 cups half-and-half, light cream, *or* milk
	1 tablespoon instant coffee crystals
	2 beaten eggs
	1 cup whipping cream
To Freeze:	Crushed ice
	Rock salt

Let the ice cream ripen for several hours to blend flavors. To ripen it, remove the dasher, then cover the freezer can with waxed paper or foil. Plug the hole in the lid; place lid on the can. Pack the outer freezer bucket with enough ice and rock salt to cover the top of the freezer can. (Use 4 cups ice per 1 cup salt.)

To Prepare Nuts: In a small skillet combine pecans and margarine or butter. Cook and stir over low heat till nuts are toasted. Set aside to cool.

To Prepare Ice Cream: Coarsely chop chocolate. In a medium saucepan combine sugar and gelatin. Stir in the chocolate; *2 cups* of the half-and-half, light cream, or milk; and coffee crystals. Cook and stir over medium heat till sugar and gelatin dissolve and mixture just boils. Remove from heat. Gradually stir about *half* of the hot mixture into beaten eggs. Return all of the egg mixture to the saucepan. Cook and stir till nearly bubbly *but do not boil*; reduce heat. Cook and stir for 2 minutes more. Remove from heat. Stir in the remaining half-and-half, light cream, or milk and the whipping cream. Chill. Stir in the toasted nuts.

To Freeze: Pour ice cream mixture into a 2-quart ice cream freezer container. Freeze according to the manufacturer's directions, using crushed ice and rock salt.

Per serving: 439 calories / 6 g protein / 32 g carbohydrate / 34 g fat (16 g saturated) / 120 mg cholesterol / 71 mg sodium / 252 mg potassium.

Indirect-Grilling Poultry

If desired, remove the skin from the poultry. Rinse poultry and pat dry with paper towels. In a covered grill arrange *medium-hot* coals around a drip pan, then test for *medium* heat above the pan (see page 10). Place unstuffed poultry, breast side up, on the grill rack directly over the drip pan, not over the coals. Cover and grill for the time given below or till done, adding more coals to maintain heat as necessary. (*Note:* Birds vary in size, shape, and tenderness. Use these times as general guides.)

To test for doneness, cut into the thickest part of the meat near a bone; juices should run clear and meat should not be pink. Or, grasp the end of the drumstick with a paper towel. It should move up and down and twist easily in the socket. For turkeys and larger chickens, insert a meat thermometer into the center of the inside thigh muscle, not touching bone; thermometer should register 180° to 185°. In a whole or half turkey breast, thermometer should register 170°.

Cut	Weight	Temperature	Doneness	Indirect-Grilling Time (hours)
Chicken, whole	2½ to 3 pounds	Medium	Tender and no longer pink	1 to 1¼
	3½ to 4 pounds	Medium	Tender and no longer pink	1¼ to 1¾
	4½ to 5 pounds	Medium	Tender and no longer pink	1¾ to 2
	5 to 6 pounds	Medium	Tender and no longer pink	2 to 2½
Cornish game hen	1 to 1½ pounds (whole)	Medium	Tender and no longer pink	1 to 1¼
	½ to ¾ pound (half)	Medium	Tender and no longer pink	40 to 50 minutes
Pheasant	2 to 3 pounds	Medium	Tender and no longer pink	1 to 1½
Quail	4 to 6 ounces	Medium	Tender and no longer pink	½
Squab	12 to 14 ounces	Medium	Tender and no longer pink	¾ to 1
Turkey (do not stuff)	6 to 8 pounds	Medium	Tender and no longer pink	1¾ to 2¼
	8 to 12 pounds	Medium	Tender and no longer pink	2½ to 3½
	12 to 16 pounds	Medium	Tender and no longer pink	3 to 4
Turkey breast, whole	4 to 6 pounds	Medium	Tender and no longer pink	1¾ to 2¼
	6 to 8 pounds	Medium	Tender and no longer pink	2½ to 3½
Chicken, broiler-fryer, half	1¼ to 1½ pounds	Medium	Tender and no longer pink	1 to 1¼
Chicken quarters	2½ to 3 pounds total	Medium	Tender and no longer pink	50 to 60 minutes
Chicken breast half, skinned and boned	4 to 5 ounces	Medium	Tender and no longer pink	15 to 18 minutes
Meaty chicken pieces	2 to 2½ pounds total	Medium	Tender and no longer pink	50 to 60 minutes
Turkey breast tenderloin steak	4 to 6 ounces	Medium	Tender and no longer pink	15 to 18 minutes
Turkey drumstick	½ to 1½ pounds	Medium	Tender and no longer pink	¾ to 1¼
Turkey hindquarter	2 to 4 pounds	Medium	Tender and no longer pink	1 to 1½
Turkey thigh	1 to 1½ pounds	Medium	Tender and no longer pink	50 to 60 minutes
Turkey tenderloins	8 to 10 ounces each (¾ to 1 inch thick)	Medium	Tender and no longer pink	25 to 30 minutes

Direct-Grilling Poultry

If desired, remove the skin from the poultry. Rinse poultry and pat dry with paper towels. Test for desired temperature of the coals (see page 10). Place poultry on the grill rack, bone side up, directly over the preheated coals. (For ground turkey patties, use a grill basket.) Grill, uncovered, for the time given below or till tender and no longer pink. (*Note:* White meat will cook slightly faster.) Turn poultry over halfway through the grilling time. If desired, during last 10 minutes of grilling, brush often with a sauce.

Type of Bird	Weight	Coal Temperature	Doneness	Direct-Grilling Time
Chicken, broiler-fryer, half	1¼ to 1½ pounds	Medium	Tender and no longer pink	40 to 50 minutes
Chicken quarters	2½ to 3 pounds total	Medium	Tender and no longer pink	40 to 50 minutes
Chicken breast half, skinned and boned	4 to 5 ounces	Medium	Tender and no longer pink	12 to 15 minutes
Meaty chicken pieces	2 to 2½ pounds total	Medium	Tender and no longer pink	35 to 45 minutes
Turkey breast tenderloin steak	4 to 6 ounces	Medium	Tender and no longer pink	15 to 18 minutes

Indirect-Grilling Meat

In a covered grill arrange *medium-hot* coals around a drip pan, then test for *medium* heat above the pan (see page 10), unless chart says otherwise. Insert a meat thermometer (for roasts) into the meat. Place meat, fat side up, on the grill rack directly over the drip pan, not over the coals. Cover and grill for the time given below or till meat thermometer registers desired temperature, adding more coals to maintain heat as necessary.

Cut	Thickness/Weight	Temperature	Doneness	Indirect-Grilling Time
Beef				
Flank steak	¾ to 1 inch thick	Medium	Medium	18 to 22 minutes
Boneless chuck steak	¾ to 1 inch thick	Medium	Rare Medium	22 to 26 minutes 26 to 28 minutes
Top round steak	1 inch thick	Medium	Rare Medium	24 to 26 minutes 28 to 30 minutes
	1½ inches thick	Medium	Rare Medium	24 to 28 minutes 28 to 32 minutes
Steaks (top loin, T-bone, porterhouse, sirloin, rib, ribeye)	1 inch thick	Medium	Rare Medium	16 to 20 minutes 22 to 26 minutes
	1¼ to 1½ inches thick	Medium	Rare Medium	20 to 22 minutes 22 to 26 minutes
Tenderloin steak	1 inch thick	Medium	Rare Medium	16 to 20 minutes 20 to 22 minutes
	1½ inches thick	Medium	Rare Medium	18 to 22 minutes 22 to 26 minutes
Boneless sirloin steak	1 inch thick	Medium	Rare Medium	22 to 26 minutes 26 to 30 minutes
	1½ inches thick	Medium	Rare Medium	32 to 36 minutes 36 to 40 minutes
Ground-meat patties	¾ inch thick (4 per pound)	Medium	No pink remains (pork; juices run clear)	20 to 24 minutes
Boneless rolled rump roast	4 to 6 pounds	Medium-low	150° to 170°	1¼ to 2½ hours
Boneless sirloin roast	4 to 6 pounds	Medium-low	140° (rare) 160° (medium) 170° (well-done)	1¾ to 2¼ hours 2¼ to 2¾ hours 2½ to 3 hours
Eye round roast	2 to 3 pounds	Medium-low	140° (rare) 160° (medium) 170° (well-done)	1 to 1½ hours 1½ to 2 hours 1¾ to 2¼ hours
Rib eye roast	4 to 6 pounds	Medium-low	140° (rare) 160° (medium) 170° (well-done)	1 to 1½ hours 1½ to 2 hours 2 to 2½ hours
Rib roast	4 to 6 pounds	Medium-low	140° (rare) 160° (medium) 170° (well-done)	2¼ to 2¾ hours 2¾ to 3¼ hours 3¼ to 3¾ hours
Tenderloin roast	2 to 3 pounds (half) 4 to 6 pounds (whole)	Medium-high Medium-high	140° (rare) 140° (rare)	¾ to 1 hour 1¼ to 1½ hours
Round tip roast	3 to 5 pounds 6 to 8 pounds	Medium-low Medium-low	140° to 170° 140° to 170°	1¼ to 2½ hours 2 to 3¼ hours

Cut	Thickness/Weight	Temperature	Doneness	Indirect-Grilling Time
Top round roast	4 to 6 pounds 3 to 3½ pounds	Medium-low Medium-low	140° to 170° 140° to 170°	1 to 2 hours 1 to 1½ hours
Boneless chuck roast (shoulder, chuck eye, cross rib)	3 to 4 pounds	Medium-low	140° to 170°	1½ to 2 hours
Veal Chop	1 inch thick	Medium	Medium Well-done	14 to 16 minutes 16 to 18 minutes
Loin roast	3 to 5 pounds	Medium-low	160° to 170°	1¾ to 3 hours
Rib roast	3 to 5 pounds	Medium-low	160° to 170°	1¼ to 2½ hours
Lamb Chop	1 inch thick	Medium	Rare Medium	16 to 18 minutes 18 to 20 minutes
Boneless rolled leg roast	4 to 7 pounds	Medium-low	160° (medium-well)	2¼ to 3¾ hours
Boneless rolled shoulder roast	2 to 3 pounds	Medium-low	160° (medium-well)	1½ to 2¼ hours
Rib roast	1¾ to 2½ pounds	Medium-low	140° (rare) 160° (medium-well)	¾ to 1 hour 1 to 1¼ hours
Whole leg roast	5 to 7 pounds	Medium-low	140° (rare) 160° (medium-well)	1¾ to 2¼ hours 2¼ to 2½ hours
Pork Blade steak	½ inch thick	Medium-high	Well-done	24 to 28 minutes
Chop	¾ inch thick 1¼ to 1½ inches thick	Medium-high Medium	Medium to well-done Medium Well-done	20 to 24 minutes 35 to 40 minutes 40 to 45 minutes
Ham slice (fully cooked)	1 inch thick	Medium-high	Heated through	20 to 24 minutes
Boneless top loin roast	2 to 4 pounds (single loin) 3 to 5 pounds (double loin tied)	Medium-low Medium-low	160° to 170° 160° to 170°	1 to 1¼ hours 1¼ to 2¼ hours
Ribs, loin-back, spareribs	2 to 4 pounds	Medium	Well-done	1¼ to 1½ hours
Ribs, country-style	2 to 4 pounds	Medium	Well-done	1½ to 2 hours
Loin blade or sirloin roast	3 to 4 pounds	Medium-low	170° (well-done)	1¾ to 2½ hours
Loin center rib roast (backbone loosened)	3 to 5 pounds	Medium-low	160° to 170°	1¼ to 2½ hours
Rib crown roast	6 to 8 pounds	Medium-low	160° to 170°	2 to 3½ hours
Tenderloin	¾ to 1 pound	Medium	160° to 170°	½ to ¾ hour
Ham (fully cooked) (boneless half) (boneless portion)	4 to 6 pounds 3 to 4 pounds	Medium-low Medium-low	140° 140°	1¼ to 2½ hours 1½ to 2¼ hours
Ham (fully cooked) smoked picnic	5 to 8 pounds	Medium-low	140°	2 to 3 hours
Miscellaneous Bratwurst, Polish, or Italian sausages (fresh link)		Medium	Well-done	20 to 24 minutes

Direct-Grilling Meat

Test for the desired temperature of the coals (see page 10). Place the meat on the grill rack of an uncovered grill directly over the preheated coals. Grill the meat, uncovered, for the time given below or till done, turning the meat over halfway through the grilling time.

Cut	Thickness (inches)	Coal Temperature	Doneness	Direct-Grilling Time (minutes)
Beef				
Flank steak	¾ to 1	Medium	Medium	18 to 22
Boneless chuck steak	¾ to 1	Medium	Rare	22 to 26
			Medium	26 to 28
Top round steak	1	Medium	Rare	24 to 26
			Medium	28 to 30
	1½	Medium	Rare	24 to 28
			Medium	28 to 32
Steak (top loin, T-bone, porterhouse, sirloin, rib, rib eye)	1	Medium	Rare	16 to 20
			Medium	20 to 24
	1¼ to 1½	Medum	Rare	20 to 22
			Medium	22 to 26
Tenderloin steak	1	Medium	Rare	16 to 20
			Medium	20 to 22
	1½	Medium	Rare	18 to 22
			Medium	22 to 26
Boneless sirloin steak	1	Medium	Rare	22 to 26
			Medium	26 to 30
	1½	Medium	Rare	32 to 36
			Medium	36 to 40
Ground-meat patties	¾ (4 per pound)	Medium	No pink remains	20 to 24
Veal				
Chop	1	Medium	Medium to well-done	19 to 23
Lamb				
Chop	1	Medium	Rare	10 to 14
			Medium	14 to 16
Pork				
Chop	¾	Medium-high	Medium to well-done	8 to 11
	1¼ to 1½	Medium	Medium	25 to 30
			Well-done	30 to 35
Miscellaneous				
Frankfurters, smoked bratwurst, etc.	6 per pound	Medium-high	Heated through	3 to 5

Indirect-Grilling Fish

Thaw fish or shellfish, if frozen. In a covered grill arrange *medium-hot* coals around drip pan, then test for *medium* heat above the pan (see page 10). For fish fillets, place in a well-greased grill basket. For fish steaks and other fish and seafood, grease the grill rack. Place the fish on the greased grill rack over the drip pan. Cover and grill for the time given below or until the fish just begins to flake easily when tested with a fork; scallops and shrimp should look opaque. Turn fish over halfway through the grilling time. If deisred, brush with melted margarine or butter.

Form of Fish	Weight, Size, or Thickness	Temperature	Doneness	Indirect-Grilling Time (minutes)
Fillets, steaks, or cubes	½ to 1 inch thick	Medium	Flakes	4 to 6 (per ½ inch thickness)
Dressed fish	½ to 1½ pounds	Medium	Flakes	20 to 25 (per ½ pound)
Sea scallops	12 to 15 per pound	Medium	Opaque	5 to 7
Shrimp	Medium (20 per pound)	Medium	Opaque	5 to 7
	Jumbo (12 to 15 per pound)	Medium	Opaque	7 to 10

Direct-Grilling Fish

Thaw fish or shellfish, if frozen. Test for *medium-hot* coals (see page 10). For fish fillets, place in a well-greased grill basket. For fish steaks and other fish and seafood, grease the grill rack. Place the fish on the rack directly over the preheated coals. Grill, uncovered, for the time given below or until the fish just begins to flake easily when tested with a fork; lobster, scallops, and shrimp should look opaque. Turn fish over halfway through the grilling time. If desired, brush with melted margarine or butter.

Form of Fish	Weight, Size, or Thickness	Coal Temperature	Doneness	Direct-Grilling Time (minutes)
Fillets, steaks, or cubes	½ to 1 inch thick	Medium	Flakes	4 to 6 (per ½ inch thickness)
Dressed fish	½ to 1½ pounds	Medium	Flakes	7 to 9 (per ½ pound)
Lobster tails	6 ounces	Medium	Flakes	6 to 10
	8 ounces	Medium	Flakes	12 to 15
Sea scallops	12 to 15 per pound	Medium	Opaque	5 to 8
Shrimp	Medium (20 per pound)	Medium	Opaque	6 to 8
	Jumbo (12 to 15 per pound)	Medium	Opaque	10 to 12

Direct-Grilling Vegetables

Before grilling, rinse, trim, cut up, and precook vegetables as directed below. To precook vegetables, in a saucepan bring a small amount of water to boiling; add desired vegetable and simmer, covered, for the time specified in the chart. Drain well. Generously brush vegetables with *olive oil, margarine, or butter* before grilling to prevent vegetables from sticking to the grill rack. Test for *medium* or *medium-hot* coals (see page 10). To grill, place the vegetables on a piece of heavy foil or on the grill rack directly over the preheated coals. If placing directly on grill rack, lay vegetables perpendicular to wires on the rack so vegetables don't fall into coals. Grill, uncovered, for the time given below or till tender; turning occasionally. Watch grilling closely; try not to let vegetables char.

Vegetable	Preparation	Precooking Time	Direct-Grilling Time (minutes)
Asparagus	Snap off and discard tough bases of stems. Precook, then tie asparagus in bundles with strips of cooked green onion tops.	3 to 4 minutes	3 to 5
Fresh baby carrots	Cut off carrot tops. Wash and peel carrots.	3 to 5 minutes	3 to 5
Eggplant	Cut off top and blossom ends. Cut eggplant crosswise into 1-inch-thick slices.	Do not precook.	8
Fennel	Snip off feathery leaves. Cut off stems.	10 minutes	8
Leeks	Cut off green tops; trim bulb roots and remove 1 or 2 layers of white skin.	10 minutes or till tender; then halve lengthwise.	5
Scallopini squash	Rinse and trim ends.	3 minutes	20
Sweet peppers	Remove stems. Quarter peppers. Remove seeds and membranes. Cut into 1-inch-wide strips.	Do not precook.	8 to 10
New potatoes	Halve potatoes.	10 minutes or till almost tender	10 to 12
Zucchini or yellow summer squash	Wash; cut off ends. Quarter lengthwise into long strips.	Do not precook.	5 to 6

Index

Keep track of your daily nutrition needs by using the information we provide at the end of each recipe. We've analyzed the nutritional content of each recipe serving for you. When a recipe gives an ingredient substitution, we used the first choice in the analysis. If it makes a range of servings (such as 4 to 6), we used the smallest number. Ingredients listed as optional weren't included in the calculations.

If you would like to order additional copies of any of our books, call 1-800-678-2803 or check with your local bookstore.

Metric Cooking Hints

By making a few conversions, cooks in Australia, Canada, and the United Kingdom can use the recipes in Better Homes and Gardens® *Grill It Right!* with confidence. The charts on this page provide a guide for converting measurements from the U.S. customary system, which is used throughout this book, to the imperial and metric systems. There also is a conversion table for oven temperatures to accommodate the differences in oven calibrations.

Volume and Weight: Americans traditionally use cup measures for liquid and solid ingredients. The chart (top right) shows the approximate imperial and metric equivalents. If you are accustomed to weighing solid ingredients, here are some helpful approximate equivalents.

- 1 cup butter, caster sugar, or rice = 8 ounces = about 250 grams
- 1 cup flour = 4 ounces = about 125 grams
- 1 cup icing sugar = 5 ounces = about 150 grams

Spoon measures are used for smaller amounts of ingredients. Although the size of the tablespoon varies slightly among countries. However, for practical purposes and for recipes in this book, a straight substitution is all that's necessary.

Measurements made using cups or spoons should always be level, unless stated otherwise.

Product Differences: Most of the ingredients called for in the recipes in this book are available in English-speaking countries. However, some are known by different names. Here are some common American ingredients and their possible counterparts:

- Sugar is granulated or caster sugar.
- Powdered sugar is icing sugar.
- All-purpose flour is plain household flour or white flour. When self-rising flour is used in place of all-purpose flour in a recipe that calls for leavening, omit the leavening agent (baking soda or baking powder) and salt.
- Light corn syrup is golden syrup.
- Cornstarch is cornflour.
- Baking soda is bicarbonate of soda.
- Vanilla is vanilla essence.

Useful Equivalents

⅛ teaspoon = 0.5ml
¼ teaspoon = 1ml
½ teaspoon = 2 ml
1 teaspoon = 5 ml
¼ cup = 2 fluid ounces = 50ml
⅓ cup = 3 fluid ounces = 75ml
½ cup = 4 fluid ounces = 125ml

⅔ cup = 5 fluid ounces = 150ml
¾ cup = 6 fluid ounces = 175ml
1 cup = 8 fluid ounces = 250ml
2 cups = 1 pint
2 pints = 1 litre
½ inch =1 centimetre
1 inch = 2 centimetres

Baking Pan Sizes

American	Metric
8x1½-inch round baking pan	20x4-centimetre sandwich or cake tin
9x1½-inch round baking pan	23x3.5-centimetre sandwich or cake tin
11x7x1½-inch baking pan	28x18x4-centimetre baking pan
13x9x2-inch baking pan	32.5x23x5-centimetre baking pan
12x7½x2-inch baking dish	30x19x5-centimetre baking pan
15x10x2-inch baking pan	38x25.5x2.5-centimetre baking pan (Swiss roll tin)
9-inch pie plate	22x4- or 23x4-centimetre pie plate
7- or 8-inch springform pan	18- or 20-centimetre springform or loose-bottom cake tin
9x5x3-inch loaf pan	23x13x6-centimetre or 2-pound narrow loaf pan or paté tin
1½-quart casserole	1.5-litre casserole
2-quart casserole	2-litre casserole

Oven Temperature Equivalents

Farenheit Setting	Celsius Setting*	Gas Setting
300°F	150°C	Gas Mark 2
325°F	160°C	Gas Mark 3
350°F	180°C	Gas Mark 4
375°F	190°C	Gas Mark 5
400°F	200°C	Gas Mark 6
425°F	220°C	Gas Mark 7
450°F	230°C	Gas Mark 8
Broil		Grill

Electric and gas ovens may be calibrated using Celsius. However, increase the Celsius setting 10 to 20 degrees when cooking above 160°C with an electric oven. For convection or forced-air ovens (gas or electric), lower the temperature setting 10°C when cooking at all heat levels.